Contents

Introduction

The unique scenery of the Lake District attracts millions of people every year, but on a brief visit there is little opportunity to discover where the best walks are, or to find answers to the host of questions that come to mind in the course of the day.

This book assembles fifteen of the most attractive and interesting routes in the central and eastern Lake District, the majority requiring little previous walking experience or fitness, selected to illustrate the range of landscapes and habitats that characterise the area.

Selecting a walk

All but one of the walks are circular, starting from places with ample room for parking, but they vary considerably in length, altitude and subject matter. An initial choice of walk may be made by consulting the table below:

	FEATURES				WEATHER			STANDARD		
	Scenery	Wildlife	Geology	Local History	Fog	Rain	Snow (lying)	Level of exertion	Length (in km)	Ascent involved (in m)
1 Silver How	4	4	4	3	1	2	2	4	5·5	380
2 Easedale	3	2	4	3	2	3	2	3	6·5	225
3 Helm Crag	5	3	4	2	1	1	1	5	9	390
4 Rydal	4	4	3	5	4	4	4	2	6	140
5 Stock Ghyll	3	3	2	4	4	4	4	1	2	40
6 Loughrigg	5	4	4	4	2	3	2	4	6·5	315
7 Elterwater	4	5	3	4	3	4	3	2	9	190
8 Langdale	3	3	4	4	4	3	3	1	6	70
9 Blea Tarn	5	4	5	3	1	2	1	4	5	305
10 Kentmere	4	3	5	4	3	2	4	3	10·5	205
11 Keldas	3	2	4	3	2	3	2	3	3	210
12 Aira Force	3	3	3	4	4	4	3	2	5	135
13 Ullswater	4	5	4	3	4	3	2	2	10·5	185
14 Hallin Fell	4	3	3	4	2	3	2	2	3·5	220
15 Angle Tarn	5	5	5	4	1	2	1	5	11	440

A scale of 1 to 5 is used to give some idea of the relative merits of each walk (1 = poor, 2 = fair, 3 = good, 4 = excellent, 5 = outstanding). The same scale is used to indicate the suitability of the routes in bad weather. A low score means that the route is hazardous in those conditions, whilst a high score means it is *comparatively* safe.

An assessment of the overall difficulty of each walk is given on the right (a high score indicating that the walk is strenuous), and on the extreme right is the total length of each walk and the amount of ascent involved.

Timing

No assessment of the duration of each walk is given because this will vary according to fitness, inclination and prevailing weather conditions.

As a general rule allow an hour for every 4 kilometres and add 15 minutes for every 100 metres of ascent; this should allow enough time for a few stops and distractions.

Preparation and safety

Boots or stout shoes are necessary on most of the routes, and a waterproof of some sort (preferably a kagoul) is indispensable. Take warm clothing — the fell tops can be cold even in the summer and conditions can deteriorate quickly. A small rucksack is useful to store items of clothing, bars of chocolate, identification guides . . . and walks books! Always err on the side of safety: consult the local weather forecast, give yourself plenty of time and don't be in too much of a hurry. Be prepared to turn back if conditions deteriorate, and avoid any tempting short cuts, especially on high ground.

5

Route descriptions

Please note that cairns are piles of stones used as route markers; GR stands for Grid Reference, given to help find the starting point of each walk on Ordnance Survey maps (all walks can be found on the 1 inch: 1 mile Lake District Tourist sheet or the 1 : 25000 South East, North East and South West Lakes Outdoor Leisure maps); 'm' and 'km' refer to metres and kilometres. The metric system is used throughout: 1 metre = 1.09 yards, 1 kilometre = 0.62 miles.

The maps

A uniform scale of 1 : 25000 has been adopted for maps in the text. All features described in the body of the text are incorporated, and any walls and buildings of use in route-finding have been retained. Contours are in metres, north is always towards the top of the page, and the walking route is superimposed in a second colour with its starting point clearly indicated.

On the walk

Paths in the Lake District are heavily used and it is in everyone's interest to follow the Country Code. In particular, fasten all gates, keep to the recognised path, and take any litter home. Most of the routes follow recognised footpaths but there are several cases where no right of way exists and the path is by permission of the land-owner. Please be particularly considerate when passing farmhouses or crossing agricultural land, leave machinery and live-stock alone and, if you wish to take a dog, keep it under control on a lead.

The routes may change from time to time according to agreements between the National Park Authority, who administer the footpaths system, and the farmer. Stiles and gates may be changed too, so common sense should be employed when walking a footpath, no matter what a published guide may say.

Most of the Lake District lies within the boundary of the National Park; this accounts for an area of over 224,000 hectares, for which special conservation safeguards exist and provision for visitors is made. Wardens and Information Centres offer advice to walkers and officers liaise with landowners over land management and rights of way. The National Trust is strongly represented too, owning over 50,000 hectares and participating in man-agement agreements to preserve both the landscape and the way of life. Thus the scenery described in this book is the product of many years of endeavour and is part of a national heritage, to be valued and enjoyed by everyone.

Walk One
SILVER HOW

GRASMERE — SILVER HOW — LANG HOW — ALLAN BANK; 5.5km

From the bustling streets of Grasmere village this walk suddenly leads out onto remote and lonely fells, a remarkable transformation in such a short distance. The route includes a sharp ascent up a steep gully to the summit of Silver How and requires clear weather for route-finding on the higher ground; otherwise a fascinating and varied walk with few difficulties.

Park in one of Grasmere's several car parks and make for St Oswald's church (GR 337074) on the main street close to the river.

The tiny building next to the lych gate was once the church school, built in the 17th century and closed in 1854. Since then it has been used for the sale of 'Sarah Nelson's Celebrated Grasmere Gingerbread', a traditional delicacy still available and still delicious.

This entrance to the churchyard was once reserved for the people of Grasmere — two other gates were used by the other town-ships that made up the parish. This segregation was maintained both in the graveyard and in the church, until in 1674 the people of Ambleside obtained their own right of burial and no longer needed to

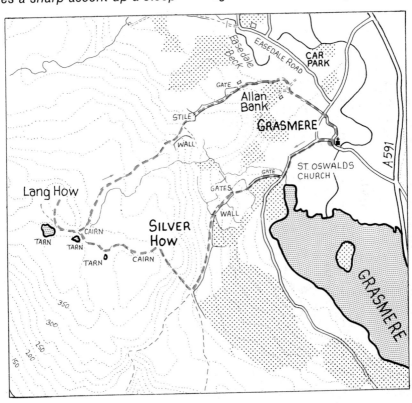

7

bring their dead to Grasmere. At one time there were few consecrated graveyards and bodies had to be transported considerable distances over the fells. Grasmere itself was raised from chapel to parish in 1349, probably to alleviate the problems of the previous year when the Black Death had wreaked havoc and overloaded the funeral system, after which there was an undeniable need for a local burying ground. Until the floor of the church was paved, burials took place in the church itself, the earth being covered with rushes. The tradition of rush-bearing to replenish the floor-covering dates from this time, and continues today as a yearly festival.

Anyone given to wandering around grave-yards pondering the headstones will find much of interest here, not only the whole Wordsworth family but also Hartly Coleridge (son of Samuel Taylor Coleridge, of albatross and opium fame), Sir John Richardson (Arctic explorer) and George and Sarah Green, victims of a famous snowstorm tragedy on their way home across the fells.

From the church cross the main road and walk up the side-road, bearing left at a T-junction.

Once the houses end there is a brief view to the left of the reedy north shore of Grasmere. The name 'Grasmere' is usually quoted as being derived from 'grassy mere', but since the lake is no more grassy-edged than others in the area it is probable that the name is actually derived from 'Grysmere', grys or gris being the old name for pigs, reared on the pannage of the surrounding woods before sheep brought a greater prosperity to the area.

The roadside is edged by young ash trees, beneath which the inconspicuous yellow flowers and pink seed-heads of herb bennet can be seen from midsummer onwards. Herb bennet was once 'Herba Benedicta', the blessed herb, harvested for its aromatic roots which were proof against the devil, though they were also used to flavour gin.

A little further along the road turn right through a gate, along the footpath signed 'To Great Langdale'. Walk up the walled track to a wicket; go through this and up the field to another wicket. Go straight on after this, following the wide path uphill, wall on the left, to another wicket.

There are some fine firs and larches here, somewhat out of place at the transition from the walled enclosures or 'intake' to the open grazing of the higher fells. The sheep that inhabit this sort of country need to be hardy; the Herdwick is the traditional breed,

Black-headed gulls over Lang How Tarn

developed over many centuries here in Cumbria but having a poor fleece (described in a 1390 statute as 'the worst wool within the realm'). In recent years there has been a trend towards the keeping of Swaledales, recognised by their black faces and white muzzles, but many of the older farmers still prefer the Herdwick, encouraged by the National Trust and the belief that the introduced breed was developed for Yorkshire conditions and cannot be expected to thrive in these hills.

After the wicket, continue uphill for several hundred metres with the wall still to your left.

There are several damp 'flushes', where plants like bog-cotton and butterwort occur, but there are also some dry hummocks indicating where meadow ants have made their nests. In wet conditions the meadow ant, *Lasius flavus* usually gives way to the black ant *Lasius niger;* this is because the meadow ant, small and honey-yellow in colour, finds most of its food underground whilst its black relative hunts on or above the surface. Waterlogged conditions soon exterminate *flavus,* so although the ground here is damp for much of the time it can rarely be completely sodden.

The path leads to a small grassy knoll where the wall veers away left. Three paths lead off this knoll — one down left, one straight on and level, and one sharp right, steeply uphill.

Not much doubt which is the right way, for the path up the 'tall rugged steeps of Silver How' has probably been worn even steeper since Tattersall's visit 150 years ago, but whilst girding your loins you might like to take in the view of Grasmere and Rydal Water. The beautiful island on Grasmere was one of the catalysts in the formation of the National Trust in 1895 — it was up for sale and there was widespread concern that it might get into the wrong hands . . .

If the weather has become wet or windy, now is the time to think about retreating for there is little cover higher up. Lakeland rain has an international reputation, and after a visit to Grasmere in the 1930s a Chinese artist, Chiang Lee, noted that 'the torrents of heavy summer rain made me think of the autumn rainy season in China'.

Take the steep path (grassy at first) that leads right, uphill, with what is usually a dry stream-bed on the left. Continue to a shallow gully.

Whilst ascending the stony scree, listen for noises like clicking stones; these will mean

that there are chats about, of which two species are common here in summer. The first is the whinchat which, contrary to its name, sits out on bracken rather than gorse, and the second is the wheatear, at home among the stones and boulders. Both birds are colourful and rakish, contrasting with the meadow pipit which is the commonest of the fell-side birds, and both overwinter in Africa.

Follow the path to the top of the gully (cairned). Do not follow any branch-paths but keep to the same line until the land beyond the ridge can be seen. From the cairn at this point follow the path up left, to the summit cairn of Silver How.

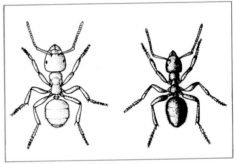

Meadow ant, and black garden ant

The view south and east is outstanding, of five lakes and a host of fine hills. The best view is not from the cairn itself but from the grassier knoll about 50m to the south.

On leaving the summit continue down a narrow grassy path for 100m to a slightly wider path, at which turn right. For the next few hundred metres care is needed to keep on the right line as the path winds sinuously around numerous grassy hillocks. The craggy face of Lang How is the objective and is always in view, but if the visibility is deteriorating consider retracing your steps to Grasmere.

Grasmere seems a world away from this lonely plateau of hills and hollows. In the slanting light of an autumn evening it can seem an ethereal place, the mat-grass shining pale silver to lend a vivid relevance to the name.

The deeper hollows of this 'mammilated' landscape contain accumulations of peat, built up over millennia by *Sphagnum* moss and containing samples of pollen from the vegetation that sprang up after the glaciers had finished their work. The Pleistocene, a million years of advancing and retreating ice, shaped the hills but left few biological clues to any of the plants and animals that lived through the interglacial periods. The 10,000 years since the final (or most recent) retreat has obviously been a busy time, for the peat deposits have chronicled a series of rapidly changing plant communities. These bare hills were colonised by birch, oak and hazel, yet they now seem immutable, an impression that serves to emphasise our own brief effect on the landscape.

The path, rather indistinct, passes to the right of a small tarn, then leads to a second, larger tarn beneath Lang How.

There is no necessity to go any further forward, but a short detour ahead and to the left will bring you to a much larger tarn, colonised — as were the others — by bog-bean, bog-asphodel and bog-cotton. All these are lovely flowers and their names do not do them any kind of justice. The word 'bog' is derived from the Gaelic, and means 'soft ground', but the prefix has lost the lyricism of that language.

During the summer this tarn is inhabited by a noisy rabble of black-headed gulls. To be downwind of any congregation of seabirds is an assault on the ears and nostrils, but these gulls are also apt to launch air attacks when your back is turned. This is in defence of their young, so if you are receiving unwelcome attention you are probably too close to the breeding area.

The summit of Lang How is a safe alternative and is well worth the scramble, offering splendid views towards the Langdale Pikes.

Retrace your route to the other tarn and, keeping it to your right and Lang How to your left, go forward on a narrow path past a cairn to bear left beneath the east face of Lang How. Follow the path as it winds downhill for several hundred metres.

In the autumn the silver and gold of mat-grass and bracken is particularly striking; the mosaic effect is a product of soil depth, the bracken requiring at least 20cm for its rhizomes. Bracken is the bane of farmers and has increased throughout the world as a result of overgrazing by domestic animals. The same is true of mat-grass, a plant of little food value, worthless compared with the fescue it has replaced. However, to the contemplative walker the merit of this hilltop has nothing to do with the quality of the grass, and this must be one of the best places in England to keep one's own company, to find the still point in a turning world.

Continue to the edge of the plateau, bearing left down a wide path.

The curious bonsai-like forest is made up of juniper trees, contorted by generations of sheep. The dead wood burns well to give a pervasive but elusive scent beloved of cottage dwellers. Juniper wood used to be known as 'savin', highly valued because it produced the finest charcoal for making gunpowder.

The path now descends steeply with a wall on the right, until a stile is reached. Cross

View from Silver How summit, north clockwise to south-east.

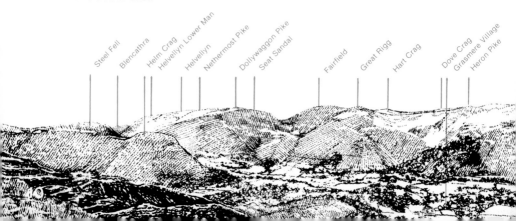

Steel Fell   Blencathra   Helm Crag   Helvellyn Lower Man   Helvellyn   Nethermost Pike   Dollywaggon Pike   Seat Sandal   Fairfield   Great Rigg   Hart Crag   Dove Crag   Grasmere Village   Heron Pike

Roadside flowers and ferns in June

the stile and go down the walled track until this opens out to a small field, at which continue to a gate. Go through this and, after another 50m, turn right along the metalled road.

The little farm has an interesting bank barn, once used to process the yearly harvest of hay and wool. The wall to the right of the roadside is well bedecked by parsley fern, a plant that resembles the garden herb so closely that it is a surprise to find the fern has no smell. Its natural habitat is the scree-slopes of the high fells, but walls must represent a close approximation without the hazards.

Continue down the road, which bears right.

The wall eventually gives way to open parkland on either side. The house to the right, Allan Bank, was described by Wordsworth as a 'temple of abomination' when it was built in 1805, but when Dove Cottage became too small for the poet's growing family he leased the house and took up residence here in 1808. 'Wherever we turn, there is nothing more beautiful than we see from our windows', wrote his sister Dorothy; unfortunately the owner of the house returned in 1811 and the Words-worths were obliged to move to Grasmere Rectory, a place destined to bring them great sadness. Allan Bank was considerably altered in 1831, so the present building bears little resemblance to what it was like in Wordsworth's day.

The avenue of lime and beech trees lends the walk downhill from the house additional wildlife interest: lime flowers attract large numbers of bees which seem to get drunk on the nectar, and the beech trees here are visited by nuthatches, a rare bird in Cumbria.

The road leads into the centre of Grasmere; turn right to St Oswald's church.

Red Screes   Grasmere   Ill Bell   Rydal Water   Wansfell   Wansfell Pike   Loughrigg Fell   Windermere

Walk Two
EASEDALE

GRASMERE — EASEDALE TARN — EASEDALE; 6.5km

Easedale Tarn, a beautiful mirror for the high fells, stands slightly aloof and fortunately a little way from any road. It is reached from Grasmere via a gently ascending rocky path culminating in a steep-but-not-strenuous section alongside Sourmilk Gill. The return route is, by contrast, over marshy ground dropping into Far Easedale under the influence of moody Helm Crag.

Start at GR 334080; this is a small car park reached from Grasmere village by taking the side-road north-west opposite the bookshop on the corner of the village square. After about 500m the car park is seen on the right next to a small housing estate. From the car park walk right, up Easedale Road. Continue over a bridge and past a junction to the right.

The bridge crosses Easedale Beck which feeds into the river Rothay a few hundred metres downstream. Past the junction on the right is a lovely old-fashioned garden with walnut and laburnum, magnolia and maple. This part of the route, between Butterlip How ('Butharlyp' on O.S. maps) and Easedale, was a favourite walk of William and Dorothy Wordsworth.

Continue past Goody Bridge Farm then, after another 200m turn left over a footbridge opposite a post-box in the wall.

The slate bridge (called Steel Bridge) has had to be reinforced to cope with the traffic of walkers; the task of keeping the footpaths open falls to the Lake District Special Planning Board which administers the National Park. The initials L.D.S.P.B. often appear in small letters stamped onto gates and stiles, but the estate work (sometimes undertaken by volunteers using materials supplied by the Board) often goes unnoticed.

Most of the wood near the bridge is composed of alder, a species specially adapted to cope with waterlogged soil. Alder is closely related to birch, yet whilst birch is the foodplant for hundreds of insects, alder leaves rarely show very much in the way of nibble-holes. Why this should be is a mystery, especially since most birch-feeding caterpillars will take to alder in captivity without any of the hunger-strikes entomologists encounter when they change the food of other 'monophagous' insects.

The pimples that appear all over some alder leaves from midsummer are caused by gall-mites, not insects but tiny spidery creatures that induce the developing leaves to send up red or yellow lumps. This is an example of very subtle chemical engineering beyond modern technology; the lumps or pimples provide food and shelter where none had previously existed.

Follow the wide track through a gate across a field to a wall.

The marshy part of the rough pasture to the right produces a flush of typical wetland flowers during the summer. The reason this is a marsh rather than a bog is that the soil is reasonably rich in nutrients, unlike those of the peaty uplands. Over thousands of years soil creeps down hillsides and deeper richer soils accumulate in the bottoms. Also, much of the fertilizer applied by farmers is washed downhill, so areas like this develop more luxuriant vegetation than elsewhere.

From mid to late summer, marsh thistles will be the tallest of the herbs; a little earlier there will be meadow buttercup, ragwort and trefoil, whilst in the spring, cuckoo-flowers will probably be most noticeable. The delicate white/lilac flowers and fine leaves of cuckoo-flower disguise the fact that it is a crucifer and therefore related to the cabbage, attracting 'cabbage' butterflies like the green-veined white and orange-tip to lay their eggs on developing seed pods.

Bog-bean in flower on a small tarn, Silver How

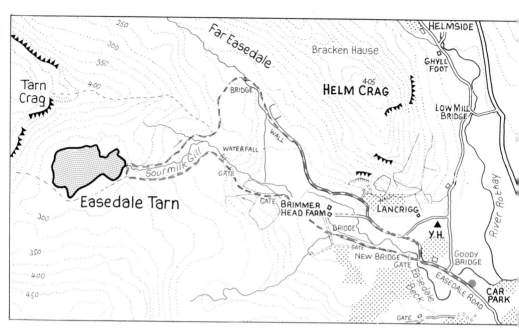

The plant spreads either by seed or by putting down roots from leaves washed away in floods — a useful adaptation for a waterside plant. Its other common name is lady's smock, but other more obscure Cumbrian names include bird's-eye, laylocks, lamb's lakens and headache.

Continue to the right of a wall, then a fence with the stream to your right.

There is in-bye pasture on both sides of the path now, the better quality grazing land of Brimmer Head Farm. For much of the year Lakeland sheep are up on the high ground where valley-farms may have unrestricted fell rights, but around the steadings there are enclosures for cattle or for ewes with lambs destined for market.

The beck, lined by dogrose, is visited by characteristic birds such as the dipper and grey wagtail. However, it is too small to offer secure breeding sites and it is left to pied wagtails, nesting among nearby rocks and walls, to hawk for mayflies on the bank during the summer. Away from the beck, the bracken slopes provide suitable territories for whinchats, and among the light woodland (even up towards the waterfall) there are redstarts and willow warblers.

Go through the gate, then cross another track at a bridge; continue on the same line on the path signposted 'Easedale Tarn', across rough pasture heading for a distant waterfall. Go through another gate and onto open fell.

The great boulders, called erratics, got here some time during the Ice Age having been transported by a glacier from their place of origin. The ice cap over the Lake District carried material in all directions, as far south as Cheshire. To the right, in Far Easedale, the action of ice moving down the valley transformed harder rocks that would otherwise have been craggy tors into rounded hummocks, like half-submerged whales in a green sea. When the ice melted — which it did several times through the million-year-long Pleistocene period — it deposited the smaller fragments in ridges called moraines.

When the climate improved the tundra or arctic vegetation gave way to birch or perhaps juniper woodland. For a time the soil was very fertile, but gradually the available minerals were washed away by rain, so by the time Viking settlers brought sheep to these hills and cleared the tree cover it was unlikely that a similar natural vegetation could ever be re-established once the primary woodland had gone.

14

Bracken, the thief of the uplands, has claimed back much of the hill grazing and restricts wildlife interest. Look closely at a frond and you will find few caterpillar holes because the plant is full of toxins. The only moths associated with it are the day-flying brown silver-lines, and swift moths. The latter, of which the gold swift and the map-winged swift are locally abundant, scatter their eggs whilst flying over the hillsides and the larvae, which look like white grubs, tunnel in the soil for nearly two years chewing their way through rhizomes and roots. But still the bracken increases at a rate of up to 5% per year.

Follow the wide path uphill; this bears left and through a wicket gate before running to the stream at Sourmilk Gill Waterfall.

This used to be called Churn Milk Force. 'Sourmilk' is an epithet applied to many Lakeland streams, descriptive of off-white arteries that suddenly appear on steep fell-sides during heavy rain. The falls hang over a hard bed of rock before descending into deep plunge-pools. The sparse tree cover around the falls is composed of ash, holly and juniper, fragments of wildwood.

Follow the path as it bends left above the falls before levelling out.

The juniper increases on the hill slope to the south (left); the only reason it survived cutting or burning in the 17th or 18th centuries was that its wood made the best charcoal. It is romantic fantasy to suggest that the uplands were a true wilderness at that time; in fact they were intensively used and managed for the greatest profit. A report about 1700 stated that 'the wastes in this county (Westmorland) are extensive and valuable. They are depastured chiefly with stocks of sheep'. Poor quality birch woodland would have quickly been super-seded by sheep-walk, and the legacy of centuries of grazing has been the gradual elimination of not only trees but also the grasses on which the sheep depend.

A last short climb brings you to Easedale Tarn.

Looking back, Helm Crag dominates the scene (see walk 3). A little beyond this to the north-east (left) is Fairfield — a peak of 873m on the southern axis of the Helvellyn range. The regular dome of Seat Sandal lies a little to the west (left) of Fairfield and

Gate and shadow, Easedale

rises to only 736m, but it is better-known by the people of Grasmere who regard it as a weather guide. If Seat Sandal is wearing a grey cap, expect the day to deteriorate.

On reaching the tarn, turn right parallel with the shore.

Easedale Tarn descends to 21m at its deepest point, making it more than twice as deep as any other tarn described on these walks. Middleton's *Illustrated Escort* of 1891 described it as 'begirt with rugged hills': their close presence and stark reflection in the indigo water give the place an austerity out of all proportion with the tarn's modest altitude of about 278m. Consult the one inch tourist map and you will find that Easedale Tarn lies at the very heart of the Lake District, further from civilisation than the tops of Scafell or Skiddaw.

Cross the tarn's outfall via the stepping stones and turn right, with Sourmilk Gill to your right. At first the path is close to the stream but then it bends left, still parallel to but further from the stream.

Common frog or 'paddick'

This part of the route is boggy; sundew and bog-cotton abound amongst the *Sphagnum* moss, and there is even a healthy population of frogs (known locally as 'paddicks') to make you more careful about where you put your feet.

Navigation across the wettest section is aided by white blobs of paint on rocks. Eventually another path joins from the left and you finally leave the little valley of Sourmilk Gill for a descent left into the adjoining main valley of Far Easedale.

Far Easedale once boasted its own little glacier, which accounts for its bowl-shaped valley cut off by Greenup Edge and High Raise to the west. Its sheltered position meant that there was ice here long after many other valleys were clear. Directly across the valley is Gibson Knott, linked to Helm Crag across the shallow saddle of Bracken Hause by a well-used path, accessible either from Lancrigg or Green Burn but not so easily from Far Easedale. Peregrines occasionally hunt the steep slopes (feeding on pigeons in preference to any other prey) but kestrels are far more regularly seen, nesting on crags that a peregrine would find unacceptable.

Bear right, go over the footbridge and continue along the wide track down the valley.

Far Easedale Gill is now to your right. As the path bears away from the stream, to the left of a wall and on the left side of the path is one of the great half-submerged grey whales of rock, smoothed by the passage of ice down the valley and called a 'roche moutonnée'. The direction of the ice-flow can be gauged by looking at the profile; the trailing edge is usually less steep but more uneven, the receding ice having plucked sections of stone from the tail.

Continue downhill along the track, now walled on both sides.

The derelict farm buildings to the left of the track are a reminder that almost every valley in the Lake District has suffered depopulation, farms having been amalgamated and families forced to find employment in far-away Lancashire.

Close by the ruins and the barn (still in use) is a small enclosure, once called a parrock (from Old Scandinavian 'pearroc' meaning a small paddock).

Only a little further down the track is a farm that survived the hard times, Brimmer Head maintaining a tradition of mixed husbandry, a herd of cattle for the valley as well as sheep for the fells. Pasture benefits from this combination because cattle eat grasses that sheep find too coarse, thus maintaining the quality of grazing. Perhaps a reduction in the numbers of cattle in the fell-side enclosures over the last century is one reason for the spread of bracken, because cattle were able to eat the young spring fronds and trample the summer growth. These days, the cattle are not of the hardy Galloway breed put out to fend for themselves, and are restricted to the floor of the valley.

The diamond-shaped pen with wicket entrances on this side of the farmyard is for sorting sheep. Flocks may be gathered in for clipping or shearing in late June/early July, for dipping at least twice a year (according to new E.E.C. regulations), for sorting strays or for weighing wethers (male lambs) prior to sending them to market — in fact, the pens are the centre point of the farm and they are rarely empty for long.

Continue downhill and turn left down a metalled lane.

To the left is Lancrigg and the lower slopes of Helm Crag, a favourite walk of Wordsworth's when he was writing poetry (the 'writing' often consisted of his walking to and fro reciting lines aloud whilst his sister stood ready with a notebook). There are several buildings on the roadside of which the Tithe Barn at Kitty Crag is perhaps the most interesting.

Follow the lane across a meadow through a gate and onto Easedale Road, which leads back to the start.

Easedale from Sourmilk Gill

Walk Three
HELM CRAG

GRASMERE — GREENBURN BOTTOM — GIBSON KNOTT — HELM CRAG; 9km

The approach to Grasmere along the A591, whether from north or south, cannot be completed without looking to Helm Crag: it demands attention. Given time and an aversion to stony slopes, here is an attractive alternative to the steep direct route from the south, giving a much better impression of Helm Crag and the beautiful, lonely valleys that surround it.

Start at GR 334080; this is a small car park reached from Grasmere village by taking the side road north-west, opposite the book shop on the corner of the village square. After about 500m the car park is seen on the right next to a small housing estate. From the car park walk right, up Easedale Road. Continue over a bridge and take the first turn on the right.

The building on the right just after the road bears left is Goody Bridge House, dated 1690. It was once associated with Goody Bridge Farm and the gates and banks aligned across the field to the south-west show there was once a track between the two. Original features on the house include 'drip moulds' above the lintels, designed to keep the windows clear of rain dripping down from the eaves.

Continue along the lane (ignore the access road to the Youth Hostel on the left), past Underhelm Farm.

John Ruskin, the philosopher and critic who later settled at Brantwood by Coniston, visited Helm Crag when he was eleven years old. His poem, written at the time, notes that its

'dark shadow shaded the fields at its feet,
 Made the cornfields wave browner and
    darkened the deep.'

Today, the fields of Underhelm are down to grass rather than barley, and the hay crop has recently been replaced by silage. To the right of the road is a silage clamp. The process of pickling grass in a clamp or silo was invented a century ago but it is only over the past decade that it has become widespread in Cumbria, mainly as a result of its simplification and increased reliability. The grass is dumped by forage-harvesters onto a well-drained concrete base, after which it is rolled, compressed, and covered by black plastic to keep off the rain. Inside, the grass is allowed to ferment at a temperature of about 100°F to produce a sweet-smelling silage; a much hotter fermentation results in poorer food value whilst a lower brew will produce butyric acid and an indescribably nasty smell.

The bright green fields that border the Rothay are heavily fertilized to produce good leaf growth and are cut for silage before the grass goes to seed. Any meadow flowers (yarrow, cranesbill, bedstraw, burnet) that might have survived in the fields when they were cut for hay are now to be found only along the road verge.

A road junction is reached at Low Mill Bridge, at which bear left.

This bridge and the infant river have a quiet magic all of their own. Rothay is an Old Norse name, derived from raudh-á, meaning red river or, more appropriately, reydhar-á, meaning trout river. At this point there are probably very few trout and the only really common fish this far upstream are minnows and loach.

Continue along the road to Ghyll Foot Farm. Go past the house, over the hump-backed bridge and bear left up a wide track, over two cattle grids and past two buildings on the right. Go up the track past both the cottages and through the gate. Turn right opposite the little building and paddock and follow a track, slightly downhill at first, with an old wall to the left. Go through another gate and up alongside Green Burn. Another gate (with a stile) is

18

passed, leading away from the stream only to rejoin it again above the waterfall.

The happy noise of the waterfall is artificially subdued, because the flow of the stream is regulated by a dam. Why is it a burn rather than a beck? The two words mean the same thing, but for some reason the Old Norse word 'beck' — universal throughout Cumbria — is here replaced by the Anglo-Saxon 'burn', a term more closely associated with the upper reaches of Northumbrian rivers.

The sides of the Green Burn valley are clothed in a remarkable jigsaw of plant communities, particularly noticeable in the autumn when the bracken is brown/bronze and the mat-grass turns almost white, a piebald landscape resulting from different soil depths and quality.

Continue up the obvious path, stream to your left, until the ground levels out before a wide flat area of marshland.

This is Greenburn Bottom; the rainwater falling on the surrounding arc of fells collects in the basin but is prevented from draining further downhill by a rock bar. The result is a mire with patches of *Sphagnum* and hair moss, bog cotton, jointed rush, sundew and bogbean. The dry hummocks — of morainic origin —, and the shelves of the mire are colonised by mat-grass *(Nardus)* and purple moor grass *(Molinia)*, another classic community of upland plants.

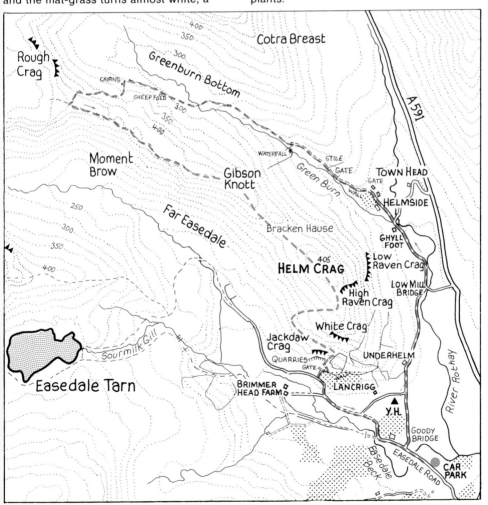

Follow the path left across the stream.

The 'burn' at this point resembles an East Anglian 'lode', a peaty channel draining level fens. Rushes line the bank and aquatic plants like crowfoot and bog pondweed provide a refuge for tadpoles and dragonfly nymphs.

Bear right alongside the mire and past a sheepfold.

Anyone who has read *The Old Straight Track* and has an eye for ley-lines might, with only a little imagination, transform the fold (based on three massive boulders) into a small henge and the grassy hummocks into barrows.

As the path rises above the basin it becomes a single grass track. A cairn is passed, then two together are reached about 50m before a large boulder. Turn sharp left uphill at the two cairns. If you miss them becuse of high bracken you may find yourself approaching a heather-covered boulder, in which case stop and retrace your steps until the uphill path is regained. After several hundred metres the path bears right and ascends more quickly, becoming clearer as it gets higher.

The bracken and rough grass of the pathside are not rich in wildlife but several beetles are to be found here including the dor, which lays its eggs on subterranean hordes of sheep dung, and the garden chafer which spends its early life eating roots. Both species take to the wing on sunny days; the former is round and black or irridescent blue, the latter brown with a metallic green thorax. But neither is very manoeuverable and they are inclined to crash into unexpected obstacles like walls and walkers.

View from Helm Crag summit, north clockwise to south-west.

Continue obliquely uphill (following the small cairns) until the path fades out about 20m below the ridge top. Now follow a line of cairns sharp left to the ridge summit which is traversed by a good path.

The view to the south is of Far Easedale, which begins wild but can be seen snaking its way down to the fertile valley of Grasmere. Beyond the lake is Loughrigg, described in walks 4 and 6.

Directly opposite (ie SSW) across Easedale is the back of Tarn Crag, above which, to its right, is a shelf called Deer Bields. A 'bield' is a refuge, so this must have been a resort of the red deer that roamed the fells in medieval times.

Turn left along the path, which is followed along the ridge top towards Helm Crag for about 2km.

An exhilarating walk along an uneven ridge; to the right, Easedale Tarn and the return route of walk 2 gradually come into view, whilst in the distance are the upper features of the Langdale Pikes.

The steep crags to the right, here and there clothed in juniper bushes, are the home of jackdaws and kestrels; viewed from above, especially in strong sunlight, a bird's plumage looks paler above and darker below, the colours unexpectedly distorted. But the mastery of flight is nowhere better appreciated.

There is a steep final pull up to the summit of Helm Crag.

Helm Crag may be under 400m in height, but it has a dramatically rock-shattered summit. The main tor on its eastern side is marked by the well-known 'Lion and Lamb' pinnacles which, even at this close range, look more than half alive.

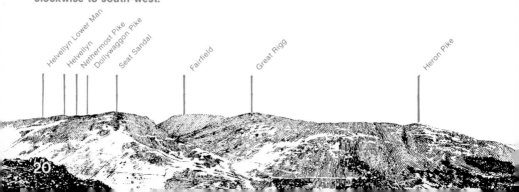

Helm Crag summit, Grasmere in the distance

The view to the south and west is excellent; that to the east and north-east, of more rounded fells, is impressive even if the A591 is uncomfortably close. The gap through which the road ascends, between Seat Sandal on the eastern side and Steel Fell on the west, is called Dunmail Raise. This marks the boundary between old Cumberland and Westmorland, but it is also reputed to commemorate where Duvenald (or Dunmail), the last king of Cumberland, was defeated and slain in 924. The victor was Edmund of Northumbria; for diplomatic reasons he handed the county over to Malcolm of Scotland, and for a century Cumbria was a Scottish dependency. It was returned in 1032 by Knut (Canute) in exchange for Lothian.

Cross the summit and go down the grassy descent ridge facing Grasmere, which provides several convenient vantage points for surveying the village.

Gray, one of the earliest tourists to the area in the 18th century, described Grasmere as being 'a white village, with the parish church rising in the midst of it; hanging enclosures, cornfields, and meadows, green as an emerald, with their trees and hedges and cattle, fill up the whole space from the

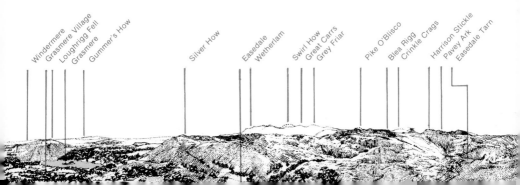

Windermere Village · Grasmere · Loughrigg Fell · Grasmere · Gummer's How · Silver How · Easedale · Wetherlam · Swirl How · Great Carrs · Grey Friar · Pike O'Blisco · Blea Rigg · Crinkle Crags · Harrison Stickle · Pavey Ark · Easedale Tarn

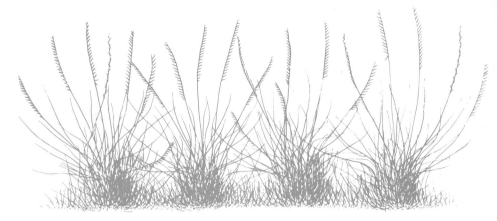

edge of the water . . . . all is peace, rusticity, and happy poverty . . . .'

The average holding for tenant farmers around Grasmere today is about 120ha, resulting in an open landscape and economically viable stock-rearing units. This has not always been the case however, and in medieval times the size of the holdings was much smaller. When the population expanded — as it did for example in Tudor times — the tenements were divided still further until, according to the Grasmere Rental of 1574, 'the wretched parcels left after generations of sub-division' were not adequate to support the rural population and poverty and hunger were the inevitable consequences. There was also a deteriorating climate (known as the Little Ice Age) and regular outbreaks of Black Death to contend with; little wonder that any remaining small-holders sold up and a few shrewd land-barons were able to buy up the area and lay the foundations for the landscape we see today.

The traditional path down the 'snout' has been badly eroded, so from the first grassy level below the summit follow the way-marked diversion downhill to the right. Where it becomes a wide stone path follow it down for about 600m to a wall.

White Crag is to your left, Jackdaw Crag below and to your right. The scrubby hill-side, with yew, rowan, and hawthorn is ideal for seed-eating birds, of which the finches are the most numerous. During the late summer groups of chaffinches, greenfinches, linnets and goldfinches will be foraging for food, a process that may seem haphazard but is in fact remarkably sophisticated, each species having its own feeding habits and preferences.

For example those with big beaks can crack seed cases, whilst those with small beaks are able to extract tiny seeds from nooks and crannies. Chaffinches feed mostly on the ground, linnets half on the ground and half in the bushes, and goldfinches almost entirely from the bushes. This explains why chaffinches are able to walk whilst all the others hop, and goldfinches are able to hang upside down from branches without falling off.

If the food runs out or if the ground freezes, the local finches will move south, to Africa if necessary, but the breeding season will find them back on the hillsides again.

Turn right and go steeply downhill, with a wall to your left. At the bottom of this, passing a fence on the left and an old stone water trough on the right, the path leads around a small quarry to join the original path.

The quarry is another haven for small birds, swathes of fern and a host of sapling trees growing out of the crevices to provide cover for wrens and warblers.

Go right at this junction and after about 30m turn right down a walled track. Bear left after about 100m at a junction with a second walled track and go through a gate. Continue downhill and turn left down a metalled lane. Follow the lane across meadowland, through a gate to Easedale Road, and on for about 300m to the car park.

Slate gatepost

23

Walk Four
RYDAL

WHITE MOSS QUARRY — RYDAL— — LOUGHRIGG TERRACE; 6km

An easy walk involving gentle ascents onto the fellside terraces to the north and south of beautiful Rydal Water, and descents to the valley and lakeshore to east and west. Apart from its literary associations this route – known as 'the Rydal Round' – includes a great deal of ecological interest and a classic view over Grasmere.

Park at White Moss Quarry car park on the A591, 2km south of Grasmere, GR 347066. On leaving the car park turn left (there is a track parallel with the road) towards Ambleside, but after only about 100m, before reaching the bridge turn left up a stony track.

To the left are the remains of White Moss Quarry. White Moss Common, the higher ground to the left, offers a popular view-point, but keep the detour for your return — you may be short of time or energy and in any case, Loughrigg Terrace will provide better views.

As the path climbs it becomes more grassy and eventually emerges on a metalled lane.

Just across the road is a little pond, very beautiful. Wordsworth is supposed to have skated on it, which would suggest it has diminished in size in the last 150 years, and during the winter a stubble of dead stems now breaks the surface. The dominant plant is the curious water horsetail, but more attractive flowers like yellow flag and water forget-me-not grow around the margin.

Aquatic creatures abound — tadpoles, whirligig beetles and sticklebacks, which make their nests in the shallows and guard their eggs with reckless devotion. There are red and blue damselflies too, (two different species), emerging from the water and transforming themselves into winged adults. They are immensely thin and wiry insects of vivid electric colours, tracing erratic and invisible threads among the horsetail spikes. This has earned them the country name 'devil's darning needles'.

Turn right up the lane which soon becomes a track and then, as it passes Brockstone House, a path leading to a wicket.

'Brocks', ie badgers, are not as common as place-names suggest, and there was a time when persecution almost exterminated them from what is now Cumbria. As with all 'vermin', church wardens in the 17th and 18th centuries dispensed a bounty in an attempt to protect stock or crops from the ravages of wild animals. A badger was worth about 4d, a fair sum but a fraction of what was usually paid for a fox. Around Rydal, rats must have been a problem too, for a ratcatcher had to be hired to control their numbers in 1686. These were black rats, the sort that had transmitted the plague in London a few years earlier. However, by 1796 the black or ship rat was very rare having been replaced by the bigger, uglier brown rat from Asia. According to John Walker, 'Wheresoever it pitches its abode, it pitches out the Black Ratten utterly'.

Close to hand, particularly lining the old trackway, are ash saplings. Ash produces its leaves very late in the spring and loses its foliage early in the autumn, but it is a lovely tree, even in winter silhouette. According to Scandinavian mythology 'its branches spread all over the world', making it the greatest of all trees, and since there were extensive Norse settlements in the Lake District 800 years ago they must have propagated the ash in these quiet valleys, making use of the strong, durable wood.

The path continues to another wicket (avoid any sidepaths to the right) and into an area of old woodland.

The slope to the left seems impossibly steep to carry such big trees, but their roots spread wide and help to hold the scree firm. Here and there are fallen giants, often

24

wych elm that have succumbed to the fatal fungus, but in such a geriatric wood there are many other casualties that have simply grown too old and top-heavy. The dominant species are oak and ash, the latter trees barely recognisable here in their declining years. Ash logs make the best firewood, ('worth their weight in gold', according to the old rhyme), and this fate would have befallen most of them were this wood not owned by the National Trust, who own most other old woods in the valley and whose motives are not purely economic. At some stage they will need to underplant with young trees.

The path leaves the wood at another gate to the left, and continues across open fields through several more gates.

The woodland is now to the left, enclosed by a massive stone wall. Beyond this are the slopes of Nab Scar and the wilderness area of Rydal Fell — once an extensive deer park requiring an uncompromising boundary wall. To the right, above the lake shore, is an area of pasture, the fields once bearing names like Great Nab, Great Frith, and Nab Close. Although they have been used as rough grazing for many years they are recorded on the 1840 map of Rydal Hall Demesne as meadow or arable, so it is possible that they contained oats or barley at that time.

The name Rydal may mean rye-dale or valley of the rye, in which case this less-usual crop (introduced by the Romans) would have appeared in the second or third centuries AD, a period of rapid forest clearance. More likely, the name Rydal comes from 'rudh-dalr', a clearing in the forest, used for grazing and a few fields of oats. The fields are now pasture, and even the rearing of stock has diminished — note the state of the cattle trough and the encroachment of bracken over the fields. The most important industry today is indicated by the state of the path; walkers on the hoof are more essential to the well-being of the Lake District than any farmstock.

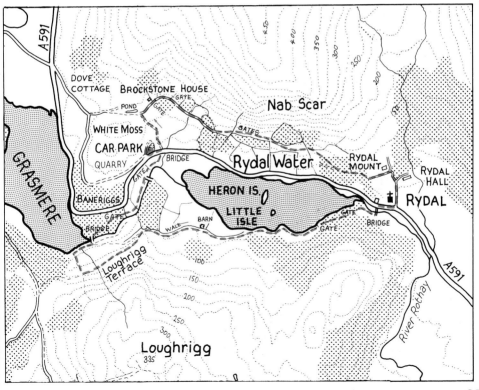

beetle on the wing up here: it is stout and docile, and has brown wing-cases and a metallic-green thorax. In gardens it is a pest, its larvae selecting and demolishing the tenderest roots.

This type of countryside, bracken-covered fell slopes by the wood edge, used to be the habitat of the nightjar, a curious nocturnal bird which nested in several sites around Rydal in the last century. Since then it has grown quite rare and no-one can fully explain why, though for many years it was persecuted by gamekeepers and by farmers who thought it robbed goats of their milk at dead of night. Perhaps the true reason is the decrease in coppicing (the wood uphill to the left was once Knott Coppice), with a loss of open woodland for nest-sites and the nocturnal moths upon which the nightjar feeds.

The fields end at a walled track.

To the left is what was once Little Nab, a field used as the calf-garth or enclosure for Rydal. In the spring, stock was gathered here from each farm before being driven onto the fells and commons. This was a well-organised event and all field boundaries had to be repaired in advance.

Keep to the well-used path through several more gated fields.

Gradually trees reappear, this time creating a parkland atmosphere. On sunny summer days you might see the garden chafer

The track leads via a gate to a road, at which turn right.

The large house on the corner, bristling with chimneys, is Rydal Mount. Wordsworth lived here for 37 years, until his death in 1850, far longer than he lived at the more

Nightjar

26

famous Dove Cottage (at Town End, on the far side of White Moss Common).

The grandeur of Rydal Mount befitted the poet's rising reputation, but his sister Dorothy found the comparative wealth and comfort a mild embarrassment. Perhaps the easy living dulled the edge of Wordsworth's genius, for much of his later work was a shadow of what he had been producing at Dove Cottage. This hardly mattered, however, as his fame was assured and Rydal became a honey-pot for tourists even before the poet's death. The local community, mostly composed of agricultural workers, did not share this esteem; his habit of wandering about the countryside talking to himself was considered eccentric, and they tolerated him with good humour but little understanding. One old stone-breaker summed it up with the words 'old Wordsworth's brokken lowse ageen'.

Walk down the road.

To the left is the entrance of Rydal Hall, used in recent years as a residential centre, but once the home of the Le Fleming family. The extensive Rydal estate was bought by an heiress to the Le Flemings of Coniston in 1409, having been granted to Roger de Lancaster in 1275. The family fortunes dwindled and, according to Clarke in 1787, the hall was 'almost torn to pieces in searching for hidden treasure', by Cromwell's men in the Civil War. But Daniel Flemming rose to the occasion and proved to be a skilled diplomat. He was made High Sheriff of Cumberland on the accession of James II, thus saving the family honour and making good the empty coffers.

At the bottom of the road is Rydal Church, built in 1824 on the site of an old orchard. Inevitably, Wordsworth had something to say on the selection of the site and wrote one of his less memorable poems about it, entitled 'to the Lady Fleming on seeing the foundation preparing for the erection of Rydal Chapel Westmorland'. Lady Le Fleming, from whom Wordsworth rented Rydal Mount, lived at Rydal Hall and was continuing the feudal tradition of employer/benefactor to the estate. However, although Wordsworth planted the yews and bought the plot of ground to the west (now known as Dora's Patch, named after his favourite daughter), he never liked the building.

Rydal church

**Turn right along the A591 for about 100m
until opposite the Glen Rothay Hotel. Cross
the road and go through a gap in the wall
and over the footbridge, then bear right to
the edge of Rydal Water.**

The river Rothay is slow-flowing at this
point, the build-up of silt from the lake
allowing reed-grass and flag to colonise the
shallows. A short detour from the path, to
the right over the pasture of Steps End
Field, provides one of the best views of
Rydal Water (once called Routhamere) with
its small wooded islands and open banks.

Walk along the wide path which leads through a wicket gate and into a small wood, then out via another wicket and along the lake shore.

The lake is shallow and infertile; there is little shoreline vegetation apart from patches of spike-rush, and for much of the year the lake seems bereft of life. Black-headed gulls bathe here during the nesting season however, and during the winter the lake attracts good numbers of diving duck like tufted duck and goldeneye. Winter also sees the arrival of wandering family groups of whooper swans from Iceland, surely the most impressive of wildfowl, capable of producing haunting trumpeting calls that echo across the fells and are sometimes mistaken for the baying of foxhounds.

From this angle the foreground is dominated by the islands, Little Isle and Great or Heron Island, the latter used sparingly by roosting gulls but far from ideal for the herons which are recorded to have nested there.

Half way round the lake the path leaves the shore and, rising slightly, follows a wall on the right. After several hundred metres the path climbs, past a barn on the right. Ignore the wicket gate in the wall and continue along the main path, to a junction.

The view back to the east is excellent, best appreciated by detouring left, uphill a few extra metres onto the grassy ridge.

150 years ago the mature woodland was coppice and the pasture was down to arable crops. Across the lake, and with good eyesight and a little imagination, it is possible to make out the boundary of the medieval deer park of Rydal, ascending to the left side of Nab Scar. The fence (or wall) was built in the summer of 1277 following a dispute between Sir Roger de Lancaster and William de Lyndesey, whose tenants had been allowing their animals to stray into Sir Roger's deer preserve. The result was a stiff fine (amounting to a penny for every ten sheep or five goats caught on Rydal Fell), and an agreement to build a secure boundary.

Back on the path, bear left ascending slightly onto Loughrigg Terrace.

This route is taken because of the superb view over Grasmere that gradually unfolds, but there is a direct route descending to the footbridge — a short-cut to be considered only if you are short of time. Along the main path Grasmere, the Rothay valley, Helm Crag and a crowded panorama of fells, create what Wordsworth called 'a visionary scene'.

After several hundred metres the path crosses a small stream. Just the other side of this turn right downhill, taking care on the steep path. At the lake shore turn right and cross the footbridge, then bear right and ascend slightly along a woodland path.

This is a middle-aged healthy oak wood with some birch. The ground cover includes a lot of bilberry, whose delicious berries ripen in mid-summer. This indicates that sheep are excluded from Baneriggs, for they have a singular liking for the foliage. In the south of England the plant is called whortleberry, but the local name is blaeberry, derived from the Old Scandinavian 'blaa', meaning dark blue.

After about 250m the path divides into three: go right, downhill towards the river, and through a wicket gate.

The river linking Grasmere to Rydal Water is stony and heavily shaded, good for mosses and ferns. To the left of the path is an interesting marshy area of pasture, containing lady smock and marsh thistle. During the winter it attracts snipe, which probe quietly for worms or grubs in the soft mud but explode into noisy flight at the least sign of trouble. This is probably why they avoid the area in summer, when it is impossible to avoid tourists. Across the river is an area of carr (marshy woodland) — an ideal habitat for woodcock, similar to snipe but less neurotic and distinctly crepuscular. The best way to see woodcock is to be at the wood edge at dusk when they are engaged in curious 'roding' flights around their breeding territories.

Continue along the path parallel with the river, past a footbridge and through a wicket gate, until the A591 is reached. The car park is opposite.

Walk Five
STOCK GHYLL

AMBLESIDE — STOCK GHYLL; 2km

A very short, easy walk out of the old town to one of its most famous attractions.

Start from the main car park at GR 376047, just off the A591 (Rydal) road. From the car park cross the little bridge and bear right.

This part of the town is Ambleside 'Above Stock', ie on the north bank of the river Stock. The name is derived from 'Stocc' = tree trunk. 'Below Stock' on the far bank is not quite so steeped in history but is now more extensive; unlike most other Lakeland parishes Ambleside's population is increasing, and at present stands around 3,000.

Prosperity came to Ambleside in the 14th and 15th centuries when there were three fulling mills, processing fleeces to fulfil an insatiable market for 'Kendal Green'. Other mills followed, then the tourist industry which was to replace wool as the life-blood of the town. It has always been a busy place.

Continue along the pavement with the stream to your right until the road crosses a bridge and the stream bears away to the east.

The structures of most of Ambleside's mills still survive, though it is sometimes difficult to recognise their former function as most of the machinery has gone. The first large building on the right was a woollen mill; a little way along from this is the famous little 'bridge house' which was built in the 17th century as a summer house to Ambleside Hall, up the hill to the north-east. Obviously, this road had not been built then, but a short detour along the north bank of Stock Ghyll will take you through the old corn mill, opposite a bark mill (extracting tannin), and to the original town bridge and turnpike road.

Follow the road again, past the bus station, then after about 50m turn left to cross the main road and pass behind the Royal Yachtsman and Salutation Hotels. Bear left up the lane.

At the turn of the 18th century, Housman dismissed Ambleside as having the stature of a large village, and the best he could say of the town was that 'it stands in a pleasant situation, is tolerably built, and contains two good inns'. One of these was the Salutation — it has been here for 300 years, although the main building has recently changed its name.

In 1858 Harriet Martineau — a formidable and resilient lady who travelled, wrote and entertained the literary world — commented that a tourist might 'use the sunset or twilight hours for seeking Stockghyll Force, whilst his supper is preparing', and should be directed 'through the stable yard of the Salutation Inn, when he passes under a tall grove of old trees on the right hand, the stream being on the left'.

The woodland through which the lane passes has changed little: oak, elm, beech and sycamore trees cast a heavy green shade and in the spring there are banks of bluebells and bittercress above the road and ramsons and celendines below. The Victorians were convinced that the climate of Ambleside possessed 'remarkable invigorating properties' and that plants grew more luxuriantly because the atmosphere was rich in ozone.

Continue along the lane uphill until a wide path, signposted 'Stock Ghyll Park and Waterfalls' leads left.

In her guide, Harriet Martineau was able to point out what she described as the one industrial establishment of Ambleside, on the opposite bank. This was the bobbin mill — originally a fulling mill — and now a set

Oak trees above Stock Ghyll

31

of holiday homes. In the middle of the 19th century it was in full bobbin production and must have been a hive of activity.

... 'The stacks of wood are seen high up on the bank; and the ivy clad dwelling of the proprietor; and then the great water wheel, with its attendant spouts and weir, and sounds of gushing and falling water.'

the sessile less popular with foresters. Historically, one of the most significant of these is now irrelevant: in the Middle Ages oakwoods provided 'pannage' (a crop of acorns) to feed swine — this was when pigs were the most widespread and numerous of domestic animals. Sessile oak has always been a much less reliable tree in this respect and there are years when no acorns

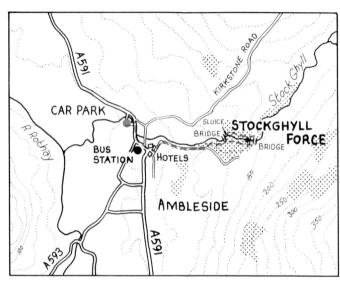

There are enough traces to work out where the machinery was and to wonder exactly how it must have looked; the bobbins were usually turned from hazel stems harvested in nearby coppices, and the manufacturers would have found an insatiable market in the Lancashire cotton mills. At the height of Stock Ghyll's Victorian popularity there was a turnstile at this point and it cost 3d to enter the park.

Go along this path, parallel with the stream, up past the old dam and sluice.

The sessile oaks are magnificent; oaks need up to 50% of the available daylight if they are to flourish, and in narrow valleys they are obliged to grow straight and tall. In the north-west of England, sessile or Durmast oak is the common species, whilst in the south and east the pedunculate is more widespread. The two trees look similar, but as well as minor differences in outward appearance (the sessile has a long stalk to its leaf and no stalk at all to its acorn) there are hidden characteristics that have made

are produced at all, so it has been regarded for centuries as an inferior tree, irrespective of the quality of its timber.

The path eventually forks; go left, over a footbridge and up some steps.

Coppiced hazel bushes form the under-storey in this part of the wood, and flowers have benefitted from the increase in light striking through the foliage — bluebells and wood anemone followed in early summer by wood sorrel and yellow pimpernel. The mixture or 'mosaic' of species that comprises the woodland flora usually depends upon the soil; bluebells will only grow in slightly acidic conditions whilst ramsons and dogs mercury prefer a neutral, richer soil.

Ignore any side-paths and continue along the main fenced path for about 200m until a major path fork is reached. The route goes up left, but a detour right gives a good view of the falls.

The rain that falls on the Kirkstone Pass makes its way either north for about 9km to Ullswater via Brothers Water, or south for 5km to Windermere. The shorter route has a sharper gradient, and the strong current accounts for all the mills, but it is not a regular descent and Stockghyll Force marks where a layer of hard rock has caused uneven erosion in the water-course. Constantly wet conditions encourage a profusion of moss — with which a recluse who is supposed to have lived in these woods lined his hut; for some reason he hated Ambleside and walked for miles to buy provisions rather than go down into the town.

Back on the main path, continue uphill and turn right over the bridge.

Most Lakeland waterfalls are blocked at some time or other by fallen trees, and there are usually dead branches and roots downstream of the bridge where they have come to rest after winter torrents. This sort of example of the power of nature, coupled with the aesthetic appeal of woodland and water, made waterfalls one of the earliest attractions for sightseers — Hutchinson visited this spot in 1773, pronouncing it 'a most amazing cascade . . . in a few steps we perceived ourselves to be upon the summit of a cliff, which overhung the channel of the stream, where an old oak suspended his romantic boughs over the precipice :— this was the only opening of the wood . . . where we could look into the tremendous gulph'.

Wild daffodils

Caterpillar of eyed hawk-moth on sallow

After the bridge bear right downhill.

The path passes several sallow bushes. How they got here is a mystery because they are more characteristic of low, marshy ground; they were probably planted to increase the attractiveness of the site in early spring. The furry catkins are visited by bees in March and April when nectar is otherwise scarce, and the leaves provide food for the caterpillars of many of our most interesting moths such as the eyed hawk, puss moth and buff-tip.

Continue to a junction, at which bear left, leaving the stream.

This takes you past a patch of daffodils and a sign asking you not to pick them. The truly wild daffodil, *Narcissus pseudo-narcissus* which once carpeted many Westmorland woods, has suffered so much at the hands of eager gatherers that it is now a rare sight. The difference between the native species and most cultivated forms is the shortness of the stem, so it is obvious that these rather tall plants have been introduced. This part of the wood seems to have been designed to be visited in April, but in fact it is equally splendid in May/early June when the oak is in early leaf, or again in October when a colourful tangle of bracken and brambles covers the daffodil bank.

Turn right before the exit to the park is reached; this leads downhill on a rather narrow path to join the main path, at which bear left. Continue close to the stream to join the path you entered by, and retrace your route down the road into Ambleside.

The waterfall is about 27m deep and is certainly dramatic, but travel-writers of the late 18th and 19th centuries were inclined to embellish their work in the same way as artists. However, although the bridge is now shaded by a group of young trees, these must have begun as saplings in a clearing created by the loss of a giant such as Hutchinson's oak.

The bridge house, Ambleside ▶

35

Walk Six
LOUGHRIGG

SILVERTHWAITE — LOUGHRIGG FELL — LOUGHRIGG TARN; 6.5km

Loughrigg, an easy stroll from Ambleside, is one of the most hospitable vantage-points in the Lake District. The route described here approaches the fell from the opposite direction however, starting on the slopes of the Brathay valley, embracing the lovely Loughrigg Tarn, and taking a more direct and dramatic route to the summit. This ensures not only a more varied walk but one that avoids some of the crowds on summer Sundays.

Start at GR 341037, at Silverthwaite car park (National Trust) on the main Langdale road about 5km west of Ambleside.

The scrub growth of birch, rowan and hazel which has colonised this disused quarry is especially attractive to willow warblers, which fill the air with gentle descending song during the spring and summer. They are a much more numerous species than their close relatives the chiffchaffs and wood warblers, both of which prefer more mature woodland. Together the three are known as leaf warblers, small buff-olive birds at home fluttering among the foliage in search of aphids and gnats.

At the car park entrance is a small building. Bear left in front of this and walk uphill to the right of a wall. Follow the wall uphill for several hundred metres.

Where the ground is too wet for bracken there are some fine patches of bog asphodel and cross-leaved heath; where the soil is too thin, especially around rock outcrops, there are cushions of thyme. Anyone versed in herb-lore will be aware of the anti-biotic claims for thyme, but walkers with sore throats can save themselves the bother of chewing the leaves — it doesn't seem to work!

The rocks are clothed in lichens and English stonecrop, a close relative of the yellow stonecrop of old roofs and walls, noted for its curious country name 'welcome-home-husband-though-never-so-drunk'. The English stonecrop produces its white/pink flowers in the middle of summer but its

Sheep and sunbather on the banks of Loughrigg Tarn

36

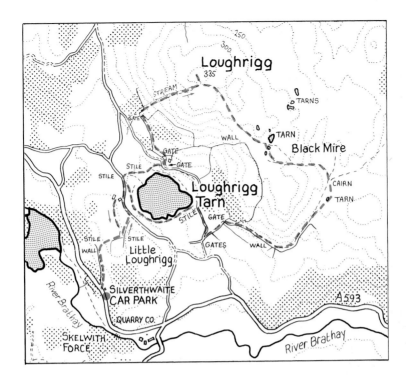

fleshy, succulent leaves persist throughout the year.

Continue to a path junction with a wall stile to the left; turn right along the path and ascend to a wall, at which bear left with the wall to your right until the ground drops to a four-path junction by a wall stile.

This bracken country is inhabited by Herdwick and Swaledale ewes and lambs. The most obvious distinguishing feature between the two breeds is the white, woolly face of the Herdwick compared with the black-with-white muzzle of the Swaledale. The latter breed is beginning to dominate northern England but older farmers still prefer the more traditional Herdwick, a breed originating on these Lakeland fells, probably from stock introduced by Norse settlers.

Flies, harboured by bracken, may be a nuisance to walkers, but to sheep they can be lethal. A species of greenbottle, bearing the inappropriately regal name of *Lucilia caesar*, lays its eggs on cuts and sores in unprotected parts of the fleece and the resulting maggots eat the sheep alive. Regular dipping — immersing the sheep in insecticide — is the only answer,

necessitating a great deal of shepherding. Summer work at the sheep pens involves shearing in June/July and dipping in late July/August. Dogs, of course, are essential for these activities, but in areas of deep bracken there is the additional problem of the shepherd not being able to see his dogs as they work on the hills. For this reason some shepherds encourage their collies to be unusually noisy, thereby keeping their master informed of their position.

Follow the path straight ahead, keeping the wall to your right, downhill to a road.

Ahead is the best view available of Loughrigg Tarn, inky-black if the day is still, shimmering silver if there is a breeze.

At the road turn left.

About 100m along the road on the left is the site of an old quarry — used for local building stone. The basin created by the excavations is now completely overgrown, but the marshy ground supports a wonderful thicket of herbs surrounding a small pond. During the early spring frogs and tadpoles take up residence; later in the summer, when marsh marigold flowers have withered and been replaced by meadow-sweet, and pondweed and duckweed cover the surface, damselflies and dragonflies emerge from the water and can be seen sitting on the surrounding vegetation. One of these, and perhaps the most reliable in appearance of the larger species, is the four-spotted chaser, a broad-bodied dragonfly of the *Libellula* group, on the wing from June to early autumn. Dragonflies are fearless predators; they are also territorial, so don't be surprised if you are 'buzzed' by the resident male.

Continue along the road for another 200m, over the hillbrow, to where a signposted path leads right via a stile into a field.

To the right, zig-zagging down to the shore of the tarn, is a ridge marking the line of an old field boundary or dyke. Oak stumps, bracken and foxglove are all that remain of an outmoded landscape feature. Grants are available for farmers who want to preserve their drystone walls, but often such features are considered an unnecessary liability and are removed, any trees or bushes being grubbed out in the process.

Cross the field towards a ladder stile.

It is difficult to resist detouring right to stand for a few minutes among the alders and willows on the north bank of the tarn. Its unspoiled beauty once persuaded Sir George Beaumont to try to build a house here, but he was unable to acquire the necessary land. His friend Wordsworth consoled him afterwards by visiting the spot and writing with 'regrets too keen . . . of unexperienced joys that might have been'. One wonders if the poet would have been so enthusiastic had the thwarted developer been anyone other than Beaumont.

View from Loughrigg summit, south-east clockwise to north.

The damp meadowland towards the stile is flower-laden from mid-summer, especially attractive when ragged robin is having a good year. This tall red/pink-flowered herb, often mistaken for a tattered campion, is held in affection by old country folk who remember the days when it was a common weed of fields and verges; like cowslip and primrose it has become a rare sight through much of England, part of a romantic folk memory rather than a sign of a poorly-drained field.

Go over the stile and ahead up the grassy slope — ignore the tarn-side path — to reach a higher path which bears right to a gate. Go through this and left along the track for about 200m, where a signed path leads right, to a gate. Through this turn left along a good path with a wall on the left, leading to another gate. Through this turn right up a steep stony path by a small stream.

After a while a group of junipers heralds an interesting little area, especially where the ground gets boggy. If this point coincides with a need for a breather, take a look at the tiny plants growing in the ooze: at the right time of year there will be sundew, butterwort and bog pimpernel — the latter by no means a common plant.

The view gets better with height, but this is a good place to appreciate Elter Water, always attractive in its wooded setting, the marsh plants and scrub having partitioned the open water into three linked sections, like pearls on the silver chain of the river Brathay. To the right is Elterwater village, backed by the slate quarries on the slopes of Lingmoor, with Bow Fell and Scafell in the further distance.

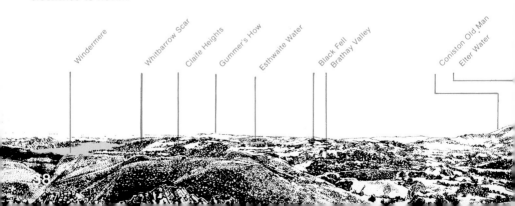

Windermere · Whitbarrow Scar · Claife Heights · Gummer's How · Esthwaite Water · Black Fell · Brathay Valley · Coniston Old Man · Elter Water

Tarn on Loughrigg Fell, Heron Pike in the background

The upper half of the path is well-cairned. Follow this to a junction by a large cairn, at which turn left to Loughrigg summit.

The summit bears a triangulation point, placed for the convenience of map-makers rather than tourists, but a convenient spot for a panoramic view embracing five lakes and a jostling mass of famous peaks. The terrain to the south is much less dramatic because most of the hills are easily-eroded sandstones and shale, laid down in the Silurian period over 400 million years ago. The northern curtain of rugged, craggy mountains dates back still further, to Ordovician times, but the rock is volcanic — hard and less easily scoured by ice during recent glacial phases.

Return to the path junction and continue south-east (towards Windermere), down a slope and through a shallow ravine.

Even the famous Borrowdale Volcanic Series of rocks suffered some smoothing-out of its contours by ice, hence this humpy ground. During the winter this can seem a bleak, almost lunar landscape.

At the end of the ravine the path passes a wall to the right. Keep left, up a wide path, past a rocky hillock to a small tarn.

The number of tarns on this area of the fell varies with the season, but there is always at least one with surface water. They are shallow and peaty and so contain little aquatic life, and the surrounding *Sphagnum* actually increases the acidity and holds the water in a spongy carpet. Technically, this sort of blanket bog is an 'ombrotrophic mire', meaning that all of its water is derived from rain rather than from underground springs and is therefore poor in nutrients. If the *Sphagnum* is constantly

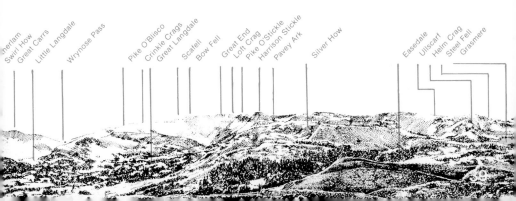

waterlogged the dead leaves and stems do not rot away to humus, and peat begins to accumulate, but at a maximum recorded rate of 1cm every 10 years this is an imperceptibly slow process.

Leave the main track at the end of the tarn and go right on a narrow path (with rocky scree on the left) for about 100m to meet a wide path. Turn left along this cairned path as it bears left, downhill to a hollow.

The valley bog to the left is Black Mire, a suitably sinister name for a dangerous sort of place. Any 'creep' of peat down the valley results in deep cracks which then fill with water, to be covered by a thin coating of *Sphagnum*. Many dogs and a few unwary walkers have disappeared without trace on Britain's moors, and their bodies may well lie deep in the peat, preserved as sub-fossils like the famous Bog People of Tollund Fen in Denmark. Fortunately most Lake District mires are small and have shallow peat deposits, but it is as well to avoid the greenest patches when taking short-cuts.

Keep to the path (ignore a side-path to the right), downhill again and past a cairn, to a level area by a larger cairn where many paths meet. Go forward in the same line to a small tarn about 200m away, then right to join a major path. Turn right and follow this path downhill for several hundred metres, alongside a wall, to a gate.

The transition from the bracken and foxgloves of the open fell to green pasture and valley woodland is quite abrupt, an indication of the separate history of the commons, which were never 'improved' but were always intensively grazed. The woodland of the Brathay valley is very mixed, still with a high percentage of oak which would have been the most prolific crop for several centuries prior to our own. However, the chances are that it would never have been mature woodland for it was usually harvested very early; even when cut for timber rather than underwood it rarely achieved the necessary 80–100 years' growth to qualify for 'navy timber', suggesting that profit came well ahead of patriotism.

Go through the gate and continue by a wall and through a larch grove, then down left on a wide track to a gate and crossroads where four tracks meet. Turn right at the crossroads, through a gate and on for about 250m until a stile on the left allows access to Loughrigg Tarn, at which bear left around the shore.

In the early summer the marginal vegetation of the tarn is at its best, when the yellow flag is in bloom. If the shape of the flower head seems familiar it is probably because it was the original Fleur de lys, chosen as an emblem by Clovis I, king of the Franks, who noticed that the yellow flag was growing far out over the river Rhine and was able to lead his Merovingian army across to safety when outnumbered by the

White water-lilies

The view north from Loughrigg towards Dunmail Raise

Goths. This may be obscure 6th century French history but it illustrates that a knowledge of 'herb-lore' can sometimes come in very handy after all, even for kings.

Yellow and white water lilies are the other notable plants. The reason they always grow around the edges of lakes is that although they seem to be free-floating they actually have long submerged stems and are rooted in mud, so they are rarely found in deep water. From the rich emergent flora it is obvious that the aquatic animal life must be rich too, and this accounts for the anglers frequently seen here. There are large trout in the tarn, apparently of wild stock, but there are also pike which survive on a diet of dace introduced specially for the purpose. Thus there is fishing by both fly and spinner, making the shoreline a hazardous place when casting is in process.

Continue along the shoreline until the point of entry on the outward route is reached, by the stile at the road. Turn left along the road and after about 100m turn right up a metalled track. Go past the cottage to bear right at the next cottage. Now continue uphill by a wall and then right on an obvious path in the same line until a wall is reached. At this turn right and retrace your route to the car park.

41

Walk Seven
ELTERWATER

ELTERWATER — SKELWITH BRIDGE — LITTLE LANGDALE; 9km

Despite its length this walk is comparatively easy and rarely ascends onto open fell. Fine views of the hills are available aplenty, but the small lakes, waterfalls, woods and meadows are thoroughly satisfying on their own account.

Start at GR 328047. Park in the National Trust car park in Elterwater village, opposite the Britannia Inn, or if this is full, on Elterwater Common. At the National Trust car park entrance is a footpath bearing the sign 'To Skelwith Bridge'. Follow this down the riverside adjacent to the car park.

The Great Langdale Beck draws most of its water from Bow Fell and Crinkle Crags, high uncompromising country, and when it rains the beck is quickly transformed into a torrent. Hence there is not much aquatic vegetation and the only stones not washed downstream are flat ones. Their green colour is caused by calcite, and is characteristic of the Borrowdale Series of rocks, hard slates forming the most dramatic scenery in the Lake District. On the near bank is a low wall to keep floodwater off the agricultural land.

Continue for several hundred metres until the path bears away from the stream to skirt a small wood.

This is marsh-woodland or 'carr', a scarce wildlife habitat composed of alder and willow trees with a rich carpet of tall swamp plants like meadowsweet and yellow flag.

The reason this type of woodland is uncommon is that it is transitional between open water and forest, and we don't usually allow nature to finish the job of reclamation without artificial drainage and a swift turnover to agriculture. Standing in carr-woodland at midsummer is to be cosseted in a green bower, breathing a damp fug, surrounded by a limitless array of insects; irresistible to naturalists!

On the path-side are characteristic northern shrubs, guelder rose and bird cherry. The latter is inconspicuous but interesting; its pretty flowers only last a few days in May/June, and the leaves are stripped by thousands of small ermine caterpillars. These live in communal silken 'tents' and their forays quickly leave the shrub looking like a bunch of dead branches shrouded in cob-webs, but fortunately the larvae pupate and the bird cherry is able to put out a replacement set of leaves to serve for the rest of summer.

Eventually the path forks; keep right, with Elter Water visible through the trees, and leave the wood via a wicket gate.

The view to the right is enchanting; the shallow lake (containing 'a prodigious number of eels') is ringed by reeds, gradually encroaching and destined one day to meet in the middle.

The name Elter Water is probably derived from Old Norse, the first element from 'elpt', meaning swan and the second from 'vatn' meaning lake. The swan that the Irish/Scandinavian settlers were used to seeing here was the whooper swan, a winter visitor from Iceland, rather than the resident mute swan of the south; the latter benefitted from royal patronage but was quite rare away from protected waters.

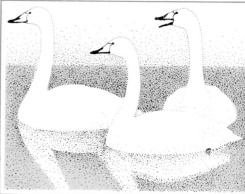

Whooper swans

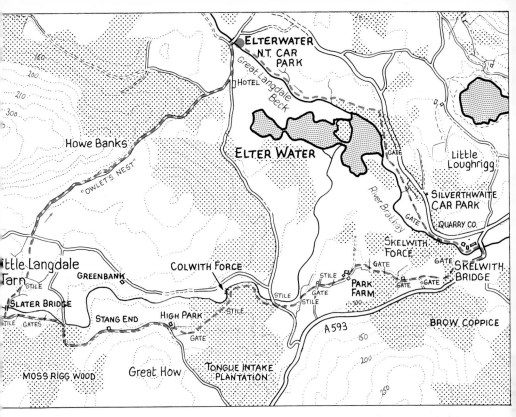

Behind the lake, and the woodland at its base, is Lingmoor Fell (see walk 9), whilst in the distance to the right (6km, to the north-west) are the Langdale Pikes.

Follow the grassy path, at first parallel with the river, then making for the left side of a tree-covered knoll.

The river, draining Elter Water and feeding Windermere to the south-east, is the Brathay, at this point slow-flowing and edged with yellow water-lilies.

Rocky knolls of the type found here, usually called 'howes' if they achieve any local notoriety, are pockets of hard rock left when the great ice-sheets were wearing away their surroundings (the last one, the Devensian, peaked about 18,000 years ago). In this case the end of the glaciation resulted in the flooding of the valley, and the silting and gradual deposition around the lake has left a level and fertile surface ideal for farmland.

Past the knoll, continue for about 200m straight ahead, to a gate. Go through this and along the path overlooking the river.

To the right is Skelwith Force, reputed to carry a larger volume of water than any other waterfall in the district. Just upstream, the flow was once harnessed to drive a bobbin mill.

For a better view cross the small bridge and stand on one of the rock outcrops just downstream of the main fall.

Back on the path, keep parallel with the river and walk through the yard of the Kirkstone Greenslate Quarry Co.

Slabs of dressed stone will probably be lying around, and one of the cutting or facing machines may be working in the buildings. The process requires a lot of water and a good deal of patience.

At the main road (the A593) turn right, over Skelwith Bridge. Continue to bear right up the hill for about 100m to a footpath sign on the right labelled 'Colwith Bridge'. Go along the metalled track for about 50m to a wicket gate on the left (signed 'Colwith'), and then through this and up into a wood.

This is a narrow neck of woodland linked to

Brow Coppice, dominated by oak and birch and containing characteristic birds such as the very beautiful pied flycatcher.

Go through a wicket gate out of the wood and across a field to join a farm track. Turn right along the track, past a cottage and adjoining barn on the right. Go through the wicket gate and across a field.

The route goes through a Victorian kissing wicket, between the overgrown 'footings' of what was once an old enclosure wall. To the right, heavily wooded, the Elter Water basin is hemmed in by Lingmoor Fell to the west, Loughrigg Fell to the east, and Silver How to the north. In the further distance and exactly north of this point, is Helvellyn.

Continue to a five-bar gate. Go through this and past the caravans, uphill along a track. This leads through Park Farm.

A far from typical steading but full of fascinating detail — such as the alphabet stone in the wall to the left.

The footpath leads between two outbuildings to the right. Continue through two wall-stiles and onto a hedged path.

The old hedge-line to the left reveals hazel as the original boundary tree, possibly planted but more likely left from an old thicket or coppice. Hazel was an extremely valuable resource, right up to the last century — and as late as 1947 there were still over 40,000 hectares of coppice in Britain. This was because a crop of poles could be taken every ten or so years and made into hurdles and fences, bobbins and baskets, and cobnuts could be harvested from the older bushes. Doubtless because it was such a useful tree it was known and used from the earliest times too by Mesolithic hunter-gatherers, ancient tribes whose very survival was based on a knowledge of wild plants. Inevitably it quickly gained magical associations, such as the fact that the unripe nuts are protected by unfriendly boggarts or fairies called Melsh Dick, but that a branch of the tree will protect you from being kidnapped and taken to fairyland. These days hazel bushes are a forgotten part of our heritage; they make poor hedges and along the pathway here they have been replaced by Forsythias.

A few metres further along is a stile; cross this and the metalled lane to a wicket gate, after which bear left, downhill.

Ahead on the skyline are the Furness Fells, Coniston Old Man and Wetherlam.

The path continues steeply downhill, over two stiles through woodland with the river below to the right, then across a small field to a road.

The little meadow is composed of several 'wild' grasses such as crested dog's tail and sweet vernal; the latter is the species that gives old haystacks their beautiful rich scent, so evocative of summer. Recent investigation has revealed that the plant contains carcinogenic chemicals, so don't be tempted into the rustic tradition of chewing grass stems as you 'jog on, the footpath way, And merrily hent the stile -a' (Shakespeare, who wrote these words, knew his herbs but was obviously no hillwalker).

Turn right along the road and about 20m before the bridge take the stile on the left, signed 'High Park/Colwith Force'.

The Brathay marks the old border between Lancashire and Westmorland, and it was over Colwith Bridge that Pigling Bland escaped from the suspicious grocer in Beatrix Potter's story.

Behind the stile the path forks, one uphill, the other to the right. Either leads through a wood to Colwith Force.

The view of the sequence of falls is obscured by trees, and old etchings suggest it has never offered itself easily to public gaze. The wood, called 'Tongue Intake Plantation' is composed of sessile oaks, carpeted during the summer by cow-wheat, a fine-leaved plant with yellow, trumpet-shaped flowers, belonging to a group of 'hemi-parasites' that obtain a portion of their food from the roots of other plants.

Doubtless the vegetation has changed over the past two centuries; Dorothy Wordsworth recorded in her Journal that she and William had walked to Brathay by Little Langdale, and found the place ('Colath') 'wild and interesting, from the peat carts and peat gatherers — the valley all perfumed with gale and wild thyme. The wood about the waterfall veined with rich yellow Broom'.

Continue, with the river on the right. Go over a stile and keep to the main path, which bears away from the river, uphill through a more varied plantation of birch

Alder and willow carr on the banks of Elter Water

and beech, until a gate leads into a field. Cross the field and continue with a wall to the right until this ends in a gateway. Bear right at this gateway and make for High Park Farm, at which turn left, over a cattle grid, then sharp right and along the lane to Stang End.

The sparse, rocky slopes of the fells contrast sharply with the green 'inbye' land of Little Langdale. On the far side of the river Brathay (the name derived from Old Norse again, 'breidh-á', meaning broad-water), stands Greenbank Farm, once the home of Lanty Slee the smuggler.

The road bears right and descends to the right of Moss Rigg Wood. At the bottom, ignore the footbridge; instead continue along the south bank of the river.

The stone wall to the left has been colonised by an abundance of shade-loving plants like the beech fern. There are also patches of *Peltigera* lichen, a 'frondose' lichen looking like fragments of wallpaper peeling from the rocks. Lichens obtain their food via their upper surface, which is why they are very sensitive to air pollution and do not grow near industrial towns.

45

Slaters' Bridge, Little Langdale

The woodland holds several old quarries. One of these, in Atkinson Coppice, was used by the celebrated Lanty (a 'turple strong, rough man') to hide an illicit still. He engaged in a profitable business, otherwise described as a 'nefarious art', always one step ahead of the excise-man, carrying whisky via Wrynose to the Duddon and returning with fresh salmon.

Walk along the track for several hundred metres, through two gates, until a stile on the right leads through the wall to Slater Bridge.

As the name implies, the bridge was built by slaters working in nearby quarries; the slightly pointed arch is characteristic of the oldest bridges in Lakeland.

Go over the bridge and up the path with a wall on the right. This leads to a stile.

Conopid fly

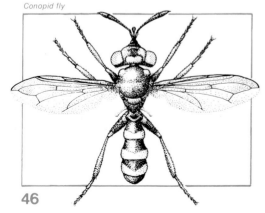

To the left (west) is Little Langdale Tarn, a shallow lake fed by Greenburn Beck, north of Wetherlam, and by the headwater of the Brathay. The fishing once belonged to Furness Abbey, although the adjacent manor was associated with Conishead Priory. On the far side of the fertile basin, well beyond the lake, is Fell Foot Farm, thought to be the site of a Viking 'thing-mount' or council. Behind Fell Foot is the distinctive rocky tor called Castle Howe; to its right (north) is Bleamoss with mysterious ancient British settlements, whilst to its left (west) is a thin ribbon of road rising to Wrynose Pass, once a Roman road linking the forts of Ravenglass, Hardknott and Ambleside.

Go over the stile and left up the lane to a road, at which turn left again, then immediately right up a metalled lane.

This old lane was once called Owlet's Nest. The dykes or walls are high and the way is narrow, reminiscent of lowland Devon and surprisingly verdant beside the slopes of Lingmoor Fell. Here and there, the wall is replaced or augmented by hedges, what Wordsworth called 'little lines of sportive wood run wild'.

Follow the lane for 1.5km (through one five-bar gate) to a road junction, at which continue downhill to a T-junction with the main road. Bear left into Elterwater village and the car park.

Walk Eight
LANGDALE

ELTERWATER — CHAPEL STILE — OAK HOWE — BAYSBROWN; 6km

Rural and industrial history are thrown into sharp relief by spectacular scenery on this surprisingly flat and easy walk. The dale head is on many people's list of places to visit, yet most human and natural history is here in the lower valley.

Start at GR 328047. Park in the National Trust car park in Elterwater village, opposite the Britannia Inn (or if full, on Elterwater Common).

If you parked on the Common you may have thought it rather untidy, not only in its topography but also in the odd vehicles, clothes lines and anomalous activities that seem to occur there. This is what commons have always been like; Beatrix Potter, who passed through the place in 1895, described it as a 'canny desolation', adding that she 'never saw a spot more strickled with herd and ducks, many of the former garnished with knickerbockers . . . .'

From the car park entrance go across the bridge and turn immediately right up the lane, the river to your right. Continue along the lane for several hundred metres until a path, marked by a large stone sign, leads to the river.

The holiday centre on the opposite bank of Great Langdale Beck hides the site of what was, until 1930, an extensive gunpowder factory supplying the many Lakeland quarries with blasting-powder. The charcoal (usually derived from birch and alder trees) came from Leighton Moss, whilst the saltpetre and sulphur were imported from India, Chile and (before 1914) Germany. The heading mill was upstream of the bridge, whilst the saltpetre house and the fire engine house were a little downstream of this point and a few metres back from the river.

At its peak the factory employed 80 people, but the business was in decline well before ICI sold it in 1931. Immediately after this most of the buildings were demolished to remove any risk of explosions from the accumulations of powder in nooks and crannies.

Continue past the slate spoil heap and towards a footbridge, signposted to Chapel Stile.

When you see how much of the slate was unusable it is hardly surprising that quarries needed a lot of gunpowder. Langdale and Elterwater slate is greyer in colour than that of the famous greenslate quarries at Honister and in Borrowdale; this is becuse the material comes from the upper beds of the volcanic series of rocks, containing less calcite. Most of the better slate is now used for cladding modern walls rather than old roofs, and the quarries that are still operating are doing quite well, both nationally and within Cumbria.

The derelict spoil heaps and quarry faces gradually develop a thin veneer of scrub or light woodland which hides their ugliness and attracts wildlife. Of the birds, crows and their relatives are the most evident, especially jackdaws which nest in quarry crevices and have little fear of man; jays are noisy but stay hidden in the trees, and carrion crows keep their distance — their nests are regularly destroyed by farmers and they can only survive by being discrete and cunning.

Go over the footbridge to the main road and turn left. 50m past the Langdale Hotel take the track left, opposite a small toilet block; head uphill with a wall to your right, then bear right until a metalled lane is reached. Go along the lane past Thrang Farm and through a gate, after which the lane becomes a path. Continue to a wicket gate, go through this and on to a junction with a track.

The village is Chapel Stile, the home of generations of quarrymen and their

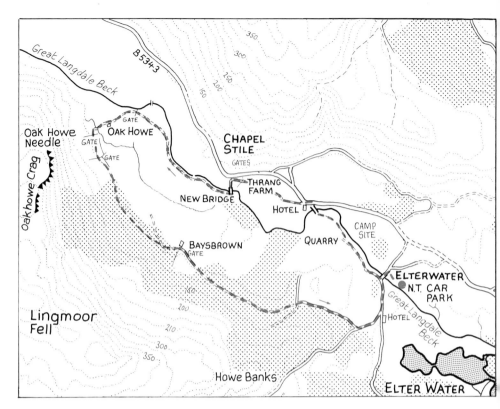

families. The Langdale quarries in their heyday employed up to 100 men, a hard and insular community much maligned by tourists and writers of the late 18th century. One of these, James Clarke, said that the quarry workers 'debauch the natives so far that even the poor Curate is obliged to sell ale to support himself and his family'. This probably means that slaters' wages were sufficiently high to corrupt not only farmers and shepherds but also the local clergy.

Bear left along the track, over a bridge.

The Great Langdale Beck draws its water from Stickle Ghyll draining High Raise in the north beyond the Pikes, Mickleden Beck draining Bow Fell in the west, and Oxendale Beck draining Crinkle Crags and Pike O'Blisco to the south. Heavy winter rain on the fells quickly causes spates capable of washing away bridges, especially old packhorse bridges built on low or insecure foundations. This 'new' bridge was erected in 1818 and has outlived others built in the area over the past century. It is shaded by one or two ash trees, and some birch and sycamores, a community of short-lived or invasive trees that have grown since the last major flood-clearance.

Bear right into a field and follow the track (with the river on your right) for several hundred metres, through several fields.

The beck has been 'canalised', its banks controlled and cleared to ensure that the water runs quickly and does not flood the fields; this flat land was once a sizeable lake, but like Elter Water to the south-east, it gradually silted itself up and was choked by vegetation. Additional drainage by fifty generations of farmers has removed any remaining wetness and the fields are now productive pasture.

The wild flowers have not quite kept up with these changes, and in the early summer the grass is pebbledashed by a mixture of meadow buttercup, a species of damp meadows, and bulbous buttercup, characteristic of dry hillsides. To tell the difference bend back the flower heads and look at the sepals (the old bud cases) grouped beneath the petals. If they are bent tightly back against the stem then the plant

48

is a bulbous buttercup, but to the farmers the difference is immaterial — all buttercups are poisonous to stock.

Eventually the track bears away from the river; follow this route which leads to a gate.

Ahead, the Langdale valley continues for several more kilometres before separating into Oxendale and Mickleden. The latter valley, bearing north-west, leads to the highest mountains in England over which clouds, bringing rain and snow, often hang ominously; it is possible to visualise how a great glacier pushed down to carve out the major valley along weakened joint planes.

The Langdale Pikes provide the showpiece, however, a combination of volcanic tuffs and rhyolite accounting for the dramatic crags and precipitous screes. On the very top, between Pike O'Stickle to the left and Harrison Stickle to the right, is the grassland habitat of our sole arctic-alpine butterfly, the mountain ringlet, which flies only on sunny days but has managed to survive as a British species longer than any other.

Oak Howe, Langdale

Beneath Pike O'Stickle, at the top of the scree, is the famous Neolithic axe factory where rough-hewn axe-heads were collected and shaped before being transported to the Cumbrian coast for final polishing. It is tempting to think that Neolithic or Bronze Age farmers tilled the rich soil of the valley floor too, but there is no definite evidence of this and it is probable that the ground was still water-logged and did not reward early attempts at drainage.

Go through the gate and bear left, to a cottage.

The rocky knoll is called Oak Howe, 'howe' meaning a hillock that might have born an old hill fort, settlement or burial. The once-sizeable farm, which had an enclosure of arable land immediately to the south-east, is now derelict and all that remains in use is a barn and a holiday cottage.

At the cottage keep left by a wall and continue past the barn and solitary yew tree; the path goes over a small stream 100m from the cottage.

Ahead are the screes of Oakhowe Crag; Oak Howe Needle marks its northern point and the limit of Lingmoor Fell. Birch and ash trees have established themselves in the old enclosures or 'intake', hill grazing first established in the 18th or 19th centuries to cope with increasing numbers of sheep whilst the better 'inbye' land was used for hay and winter grazing. The increase in trees is the result of a temporary decrease in grazing, possibly when the farm was first deserted.

Bear left along the stony, wet path; this leads to a gate.

The constant wetness of the ground, evident even in drought years like 1984, comes from 'flushes' or isolated springs which bring dissolved minerals to the surface. The combination of water and slightly richer soil accounts for the greener plant growth and the presence of butter-wort amongst the bog cotton and *Sphagnum*.

Continue, with the wall on your left, past a sheep-fold to another gate.

Coppiced hazel

Small folds or pens were important for the gathering and sorting of sheep between the enclosed land and commons. This gathering took place a lot more often than might be expected, not only for market but also for regular seasonal activities like shearing and salving. The latter process involved daubing the poor beasts with a mixture of tar and butter to protect them from, and keep them free of pests and disease (this was before dipping was invented). The men who did the job were often specially skilled and went from farm to farm in much the same way as contractors today combine corn, but local shepherds took part in the exercise too; the Sunday after salving was reserved for the godly and those able to transcend the over-powering stink of the farming congregation as they assembled in church.

Follow the same line through a wood on a wide track to a metalled lane.

A century ago, woodland was cropped for a variety of uses. Oak, the dominant tree to the right of the path, was always the most valuable whether for a short-term harvest (for tannin) or as a timber crop. In much of Westmorland the prime demand was for tannin to supply the leather industry of Lancashire and this meant that the trees never reached maturity. According to Bishop Llandaff in a report to the Board of Agriculture at the beginning of the 19th century, oak branches were peeled as soon as they had attained the thickness of a man's thumb, with the result that

> 'It is an extraordinary thing to see any tree left to stand for timber in these underwoods, the high price of bark being a temptation to cut the whole down.'

To the left of the path grow larches, alien trees introduced as a timber crop and despised by early conservationists, but planted now in small groves to enhance the hills and epitomising the Lakeland country-side to many visitors.

Go left down the lane, and follow this through Baysbrown Farm.

Baysbrown has a long but mixed history. Its name appears in documents as long ago as 1300 and is probably derived from Old Norse, translated as 'rough ground with a cow-shed'. It was once a dairy farm for the monks of Coniston Priory, but this holy connection did not protect the place from an outbreak of plague following a visit by a

50

The shore of Great Langdale Beck; rocks etched by pebbles

flea-infested soldier from London; an entire family perished as a result in wretched isolation, and was buried nearby.

The fields to the north of the buildings, on either side of the farm track, are recorded in the Tithe of 1839 as the east and west leys, containing arable crops (probably oats and barley). At that time there was no other titheable land between Oak Howe and Baysbrown, suggesting it was waste of no agricultural value. The marshy levels end at the ridge of hard metamorphic rock between here and Chapel Stile, and most of the drier, rocky ground to the south-east was wooded.

Go through a gate and along the lane for several hundred metres to a lane junction.

The woodland still exists, some of it a shadow of its original working form as hazel coppice. The stools were cut at ground level every sixteen years to produce a crop of poles for hoops or charcoal. This underwood has now been superseded by oak standards, maturing trees that will eventually shade-out the derelict coppice.

Steep wooded hillsides are an ideal habitat for buzzards, the area around Elterwater being particularly favoured. They nest among trees and crags but hunt the open fells for rabbits or carrion and are most often seen soaring high over the valley. Most reports of eagles can usually be put down to buzzards which have an impressive 140cm wingspan and attract attention by their mewing call. Each pair requires a territory of well over 200 hectares, especially in countryside with a low rabbit population, so although there always seem to be buzzards around the foot of Langdale this may be one family of four or five birds.

Turn left to a T-junction, where another left turn down the road soon leads back into Elterwater.

Oak twig

Walk Nine
BLEA TARN

BLEA TARN — BROWN HOWE — SIDE PIKE; 5km

A walk of contrasting moods, linking the finest stretch of heather moorland in central Lakeland with magnificent views of the Langdale Pikes, Bow Fell, Crinkle Crags and Wetherlam, and finishing with a quiet valley circuit touching the shores of romantic Blea Tarn. A longer walk than it looks, with a sharp ascent to Brown Howe, but quite unique.

Start at the National Trust car park near Blea Tarn, GR 296044, on the road connecting Great Langdale and Little Langdale. From the car park turn right and walk along the road towards Bleatarn House.

Ahead are the Langdale Pikes; the buttresses of Loft Crag and Thorn Crag are in evidence between Pike O'Stickle and Harrison Stickle.

To the right of the road as you walk north is a small bog or 'moss' with patches of bog-cotton, jointed rush and asphodel. The ground level is well above that of the road and water seems to be defying gravity, held in the spongy tissue of *Sphagnum* moss. As the cushions of moss grow upwards, the dead leaves and stems mummify into peat; the normal breakdown of plant remains to humus is prevented by the waterlogged conditions and acidity, and by the anti-biotic properties of the *Sphagnum*.

100m before Bleatarn House turn sharp right up a faint grass track, leading uphill by a little ravine.

Ash tree beneath Lingmoor

The steep lower slopes of the fell have been enclosed as pasture; bracken was once controlled by the grazing of cattle (which trample the stems) and by its harvesting as a litter for bedding, but today it spreads apace wherever there are brown-earth soils of good agricultural potential. Some farmers try to control the weed with herbicide sprays, but these enclosures have been cut by machine, a long-term solution which may look less than successful but keeps the bracken in check and the grazing adequate for sheep.

Continue uphill with the ravine on your left, through a gap in a wall.

Once out of the old enclosure the bracken cover becomes almost total. Even before it sends up new fronds in the late spring the old undecayed stems, full of tannin and cyanide, inhibit most other plants from putting on any kind of show.

In the cleft of the little ravine are birch and willow trees, and since the first main crag to the south is called Birk Knott ('birk' = birch) it can be assumed that birch — probably downy birch rather than silver birch — was once widespread even on the lower slopes of the fell. Higher up along the ravine are larches, tolerant of alpine slopes (the native range of the European Larch is centred on the Alps and Carpathians), but for some reason the seeds usually fail to germinate in this country and the tree has to be specially planted.

Fir club-moss

53

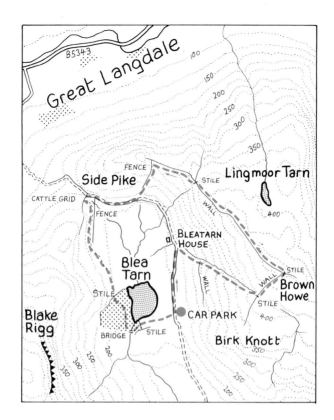

The path now wanders up through small rocky outcrops. Occasional cairns mark the way, but if in doubt keep ascending, bearing left and parallel with the ravine.

Three different kinds of club-moss are to be found on the path-side and among the rocks: stag's horn and fir club-moss resemble giant, tough-stemmed hair-moss, whilst alpine club-moss looks like tufts of flattened and plaited string. Club-mosses are primitive and mysterious upland plants and southern botanists go into raptures about them. To the right the view of Blea Tarn inspired Wordsworth to describe the col as

'A lowly vale, and yet uplifted high
 Among the mountains . .'

View from ridge of Lingmoor Fell, south-west clockwise to north.

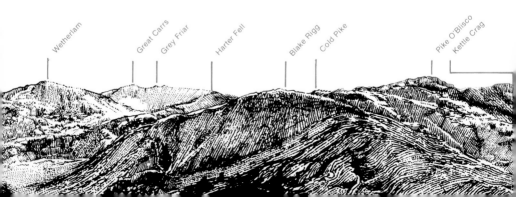

Blea Tarn in mid-winter; bad weather obscures the Langdale Pikes

His accompanying lines — part of *The Excursion* — suggest that the place has altered little over the best part of two centuries; the only real change is that the 'treeless nook, with two green fields' now has a plantation, and nitrogenous fertilisers have increased the greenness to the extent that the 'liquid pool' looks like a giant rain-puddle on a lawn. But still beautiful. In the distance to the south-west is Wetherlam,

whilst closer to hand to the west, above Wrynose Fell, is Pike O'Blisco.

Bear left before a wall and cross the bed of the ravine by a group of larches.

The funnelling effect of the wind has deformed many of these larches and some are dead or dying. In the late summer bright orange toadstools, broad-stemmed

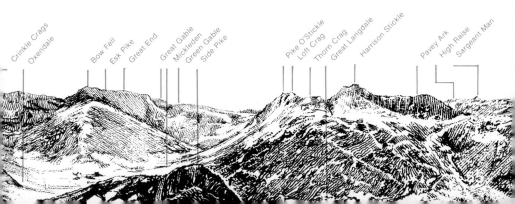

Lingmoor Fell, Crinkle Crags and the Langdale Pikes in the distance

with sponge-like pores on the underside of the cap, grow beneath the trees. These are the larch bolete, supposedly edible, but the closely related devil's bolete is deadly so take no chances!

The bed of the ravine opens out to a shallow bowl of *Sphagnum* with bog cotton and cranberry. There are also carpets of hair-moss, a plant once used by Eskimos who cut it into strips and rolled it up for use as a lightweight mattress.

Go over the stile to the right and bear left uphill, parallel with a wall, past several cairns and over a stile to the summit of Brown Howe.

A fine view: to the north-east and east is Great Langdale (a fascinating perspective if you have already been on walk 8); to the south the lakes and low, wooded hills of old Lancashire 'Beyond the Sands', as this area was known to the people of the industrial north-west beyond Morecambe Bay.

From the summit walk north-west along the ridge, with a wall to your left.

In August the dense carpet of heather is alive with the deep droning of bumble bees; there are some hive bees too, but the moor is not very accessible for bee keepers' lorries, and the traditional northern activity of transporting hives to the hills is less widespread here than in the Pennines, where heather honey is one of the great luxuries.

Across the hummocky plateau to the right, described by Wordsworth as 'a dreary plain' but in fine weather a fascinating place, is Lingmoor Tarn. It is a lovely and little-frequented pool full of interesting aquatic plants (water lobelia, yellow water lily, floating bur-reed), patrolled by a colourful assembly of dragonflies (black and common darter, common hawker, emerald damselfly). Just the place to detour for a picnic.

Back on the path, continue for several hundred metres until a cairn is reached on a small rocky knoll.

This is perhaps the finest vantage point to study the Langdale Pikes and the network of stony, dusty paths that make the ascents out of Langdale so wearysome. There is also an excellent view of Mickleden and Oxendale, the rugged valleys that are the gateway to England's highest hills. Beyond the headwaters of the valleys, Crinkle Crags and Bow Fell issue the challenge, which, on a fine sunny day, can be irresistible.

The path descends steeply with the wall still to your left; continue until a wall is reached coming in from the right, to meet a fence that has here replaced the main wall. Go left over a stile at this point, keeping to the same line but with the wall now to your right. At the fence below Side Pike turn left, downhill, and keep the fence to your right all the way to the road.

There is a quick return route here along the road and back to the car park, to be considered if time or weather have turned against you, but the walk down the west flank of the col is gentle and interesting; unlike the top of Lingmoor Fell, the marshland is at its best in June or when the 'meads of asphodel' are ablaze with colour in July/early August.

Turn right along the road and continue to the cattle grid. Immediately after this turn left to pick up a good path with a fence to your left.

It is fascinating to find an expanse of marshland that has changed only slightly in ten thousand years. Forest would once have encircled this mire: pine and juniper, then oak and elm, but these 'wildwoods' were cleared by Neolithic farmers who probably settled on the site of what is now Bleatarn House. They established the essential 'inbye' fields but could make nothing of the mire, and the drifts of bog asphodel, known as 'moor-gold', have remained inviolate ever since. The only recorded use of its profligate beauty is as an orange or saffron hair-dye, a far remove from the harsh essentials of rural life.

Continue along the path to the western corner of Blea Tarn, go over a stile and, ignoring the uphill right fork, go down left through a small wood.

The path tunnels its way beneath conifers and rhododendron. Pines were planted on the lower slopes of Blake Rigg by Bishop Llandaff, an influential agricultural innovator of the late 18th century. Unfortunately most of the original trees found the conditions too austere and more recent attempts at

Boletus toadstool

planting of alien species such as spruce and rhododendron have not been so enlightened.

Rhododendron was introduced into Britain as recently as 1763 and became such an essential component of the Victorian land-scape that it was planted far and wide, even deep in the wilderness of Westmorland. Over the last few decades conservationists and farmers have been trying to reverse the process, having discovered that the elegant 'rose-bay' is in fact a ruinous weed capable of destroying wildlife habitats and taking over good agricultural land. Unfortunately rhododendron is virtually impossible to eradicate quickly — the only solution is, as in this case, to plant conifers and let them blot out the light for a few decades.

Small birds like coal tits and goldcrests find conifers a welcome refuge, though in severe weather they are forced down into the larger woods and forests of the main valleys, Langdale and the Duddon.

At the end of the rhododendron 'tunnel' turn left over a footbridge and then a stile.

Blea Tarn is accessible for the first time to the left; apart from its western shore it lacks shelter and shade from sun or rain, and is not as attractive in isolation as Lingmoor Tarn. However, like many priceless jewels its fame lies in its setting, and the reputation of the beauty it adorns.

The path leads straight to the road and car park.

57

Walk Ten
KENTMERE

KENTMERE — HARTRIGG — KENTMERE RESERVOIR — OVEREND; 10.5km

The River Kent rises on the southern slopes of Mardale III Bell and travels 20km south-east to Kendal before it is really noticed. Its valley, particularly the cul-de-sac at its head, is a green patchwork tucked between high fells, entering the heart of Lakeland by the back door, rarely visited and brimming with curious and interesting features.

This walk follows the only route available from the village north to the reservoir; for much of the way the track is stony but this inconvenience is more than made up for by the scenery, and the return route via Overend has a lovely pastoral appeal.

Start at GR 456042, on the Kentmere village road 10km north of Staveley, by the village church.

The church is St Cuthbert's, named after a 7th century recluse who started life as a shepherd in the Lammermuir Hills and ended up as Bishop of Lindisfarne. The connection with Kentmere is tenuous; after the saint's death various parts of his body were cherished as sacred relics and hidden from the Danes by his followers, who were obliged to move from place to place to keep their treasure secret. These monks are said to have founded a church here.

Look in the crook of the old yew in the churchyard, and you may notice another tree growing, a sapling rowan; this is a 'flying rowan', the most powerful pagan emblem of good fortune and part of a faith that Cuthbert was trying to stamp out.

◄ Rowan on the rocks, Kentmere

From the church gate follow the bridleway sign right, down the walled track towards Kentmere Hall.

A kilometre to the south is Kentmere Lake, all that is left of the mere that gave the valley its name. It was drained about 1840 to increase the grazing land, but once this had been achieved it was found that the river flow was no longer reliable enough to drive the mills further downstream. The solution was to build an artificial lake at the head of the valley where the land was of little agricultural value, although the cost must have been considerable.

More recently the bed of the old lake was found to be composed of diatomite, a clay-like substance derived from the skeletons of billions of dead diatoms (microscopic plants). This unpromising raw-material is now dredged up as a black sludge and taken down to a factory a few hundred metres south of the present lake at Waterford Bridge, where it is made into superior insulation bricks for soundproofing and insulation. Kentmere Lake and Skeggles Water, less than 3km to the east, contain the only known diatomite deposits in Britain.

At the yard entrance to the Hall turn right by a wall and through a gate.

Kentmere Hall began as a pele tower, a fortified house of the 14th or 15th centuries, perhaps built to afford the squire some protection in the Border troubles but more likely to act as a hunting lodge. Three hundred years later a large farmhouse was added, followed at a similar interval by a sprawling succession of modern stock sheds and yards.

The Hall is the ancestral home of the Gilpins, one of the most distinguished of Lakeland families. Among the soldiers were Richard Gilpin who, in the reign of King John, made himself a local hero by slaying a particularly ferocious wild boar in the valley, and William, who was killed at the battle of Bosworth Field in 1485. However, it was Bernard Gilpin who attained the greatest and most lasting fame, as a church reformer in the 16th century. An epitaph in St Cuthbert's described him as the Apostle of the North who 'faced the persecution of the church and the anger of the queen for truth and duty'. In fact he only escaped being burned to death at the stake by

White-tailed bumblebee „Bombus lucorum

The hillside to the left, rising to Pengennett and Cowsty Knotts, is clothed with larches and is a favourite haunt of buzzards; like most larger birds of prey they rely on thermals for their effortless flight, and congregate where the topography encourages updraughts of air.

Walk along the road for several hundred metres to a cattle grid.

To the left is Raven Crag, sparsely wooded and with a population of jackdaws rather than ravens. To the right the very uneven, rocky pasture suddenly gives way to flat meadowland. The reason for the change is geological, a transition from soft Browgill Slate to very hard volcanic rock where Silurian meets the dramatic Borrowdale Series. The rock bar across the valley at this point was eroded but not removed at the height of the Ice Age, and for some time after this a glacier filled the upper valley, dumping its cargo of morainic debris at its most southerly point.

The quality of the grassland is affected by the underlying rocks, and the rough pasture does not warrant extensive agricultural improvement. This means that 'weeds' flourish; pignut and buttercups in the early summer give way to yarrow, knapweed and harebell on the drier ground and sneezewort and scabious in the marshy places. The nectar attracts insects, but because of the shortage of reliable sunshine butterflies are restricted to a few browns, small heaths and small coppers. Bumblebees are very common however, particularly *Bombus lucorum* (black with buff stripes and a white tail) and *Bombus lapidarius* (black with a red tail). These are able to forage for nectar in cloudy conditions, returning to their insulated nests when it rains. Those found sitting on flower-heads in the wet or very cold weather are either males excluded from their nest or workers caught out and cooled below their flight threshold.

Go along the road and over another cattle grid, past Scales Farm, and on to Hartrigg. Fork left just before the farm entrance.

A 'rigg' is a ridge or spur, so the site of the farm was probably once a wooded knoll frequented by deer. According to a late 17th century farmer from Potter Fell (a few kilometres to the south-east), there was then a 'great store of red deer on the mountains, and white cattle with black ears

breaking a leg on the way to his trial, and being in prison recovering when Queen Mary died.

Turn immediately right through another gate and up the field, passing to the right of the grassy knoll, to a gate in the top corner of the field. Continue in the same line to pass between a barn and a wall. Continue to a gate and track between houses. Go down the road (not immediately left) for about 100m and turn left just past the big house.

Some of these cottages and houses must once have been the humble homes of farmworkers or quarrymen. Today, Greenhead is typical of many Lakeland villages and hamlets, occupied by those that can afford the property prices rather than those that were born locally. However, the drift of population away from hill farming areas has more to do with increased agricultural efficiency and the search for a better standard of living than the lack of accommodation, and this is not necessarily a recent phenomenon. In the 1790s Pringle was lamenting that 'the simplicity of the ancient times is gone. Finer clothes, better dwellings, and more expensive viands are now sought after by all'.

With a wall on your right, go up the track and through a gate. Keep to the track until it meets a road.

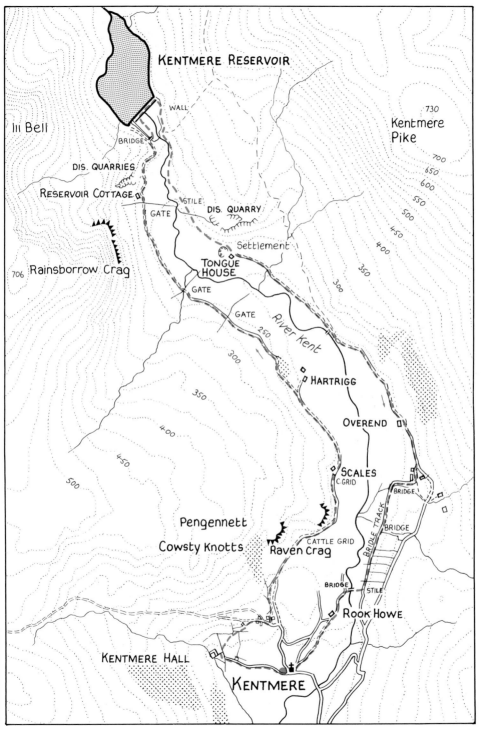

KENTMERE RESERVOIR

Ill Bell

WALL

BRIDGE

DIS. QUARRIES

RESERVOIR COTTAGE

GATE

STILE

DIS. QUARRY

Settlement

706 Rainsborrow Crag

TONGUE HOUSE

GATE

GATE

River Kent

300

350

400

450

500

Pengennett

Cowsty Knotts

Raven Crag

CATTLE GRID

HARTRIGG

OVEREND

SCALES

C. GRID

BRIDGE

BRIDGE

BRIDGE

STILE

Rook Howe

Kentmere Pike

730

700

650

600

550

500

450

400

350

300

250

BRIDLE TRACK

Kentmere Hall

KENTMERE

The road north from Kentmere, Raven Crag to the left

only on the moors'. Thus not only have the deer gone (the only ones seen now are vagrants from Martindale), but so have the park cattle.

Hartrigg Farm has grown considerably over the past three hundred years, but still makes use of the natural contours of the hillside to protect the buildings and pens. The cattle-rearing tradition of the valley has persisted too, although shorthorns and Galloways have been superseded by Charolais or Limousin crosses, and there are even a few Highland cattle to add an incongruous touch of romance to the upper pastures.

Continue along the track as it heads north-west.

The large hillside enclosures, called 'grassings', were probably stocked with sturdy black Galloway cattle in the 18th and 19th centuries, but now they are usually set aside for Swaledale sheep in the economy of farms with fell-grazing rights.

Keep to the track as it leads for nearly 2km, through three gates to a deserted quarry.

Most slate quarries closed abruptly when the cost of extraction and haulage outpaced the diminishing demand, with the result that they now have an atmosphere of the Marie Celeste.

Looking up to the head of the valley, the horseshoe of peaks includes Froswick, Mardale III Bell and Harter Fell. The Roman road of High Street links the peaks on the western side of the valley and offers a dramatic but arduous walk out of Troutbeck or Mardale.

Go past the quarry spoil and around a grassy spur towards the reservoir; about 150m before the dam is reached go right, over a footbridge, then left onto the dam wall.

Kentmere Reservoir (originally known as Kentmere Head) was constructed in the middle of the last century to satisfy the needs of local quarries and to power the mills that had sprung up along the Kent valley since the early days of the Industrial Revolution.

Across the reservoir, the wedge of Lingmell

End separates Lingmell Gill on the right from the river Kent on the left. From its remote origins high up around Hall Cove the Kent descends 600m before reaching Kendal, making it one of the fastest-flowing rivers in England. The force of the current was harnessed at places like Staveley by mills producing woollens, cotton, bobbins, snuff and gunpowder.

Walk across the dam wall and turn down the path by the stream at the end of the dam, at first to the left of an old wall, then a few metres above the stream.

Compared with the lower valley the wildlife of the headwater is very limited, reflecting the harsher conditions. The reservoir is stone-sided and shelves steeply, attracting few duck other than an occasional goldeneye or merganser. The fells are bare and inhospitable too, and the only bird sounds to be heard are the thin 'zeep' of meadow pipits and the resonant, gutteral croaks of ravens high on the crags.

The stone sheep pen on the far bank of the embryonic river is called the 'wether fold', built to gather and sort young male sheep (or 'wethers') off the hillside before driving them down the valley to market. The 'gimmers', young females, are kept on the hillside to augment a nucleus of breeding ewes. The ability of sheep to learn the best grazing pattern within the limits of their particular territory, or 'heaf', is essential to their survival and to the success of a farm, so when farms change hands the 'heafted' flock of ewes is usually part of the deal.

Continue downstream with spoil heaps to the left.

The Kent has a very regular flow, controlled by sluices at the foot of the dam. The absence of winter floods and summer droughts means that vegetation can grow virtually to the water's edge.

Just beyond the spoil heaps is the associated quarry, angled into the hillside to exploit the best quality slate. Sheep have been unable to reach any vegetation developing on the cliff faces, and the resulting habitat of bushes and rock crevices has proved ideal for wrens and pied wagtails.

Continue to a wall-stile by a gate, go over this and follow a good track across the fields away from the river.

The main feature ahead is Tongue House and its huddle of pines, but before this is reached the path skirts the perimeter of an ancient settlement, almost invisible unless the lines of its circular huts and walls are picked out by bracken or by oblique winter sunshine. The settlement probably dates back nearly 2,000 years; the clearance of primary woodland in the Lake District began 5,000 years ago when Neolithic farmers first brought their stock and crops to the area, but it was a slow and patchy process and some isolated valleys were colonised very much later.

This Romano-British settlement may have succeeded a previous Iron Age community and so benefitted from their efforts, but the increasing population would have necessitated more clearance of wildwood, resulting in the first indelible stamp of man on his environment.

Go through the gated yard past Tongue House.

The farm building has been derelict for many years, and its fate will depend on the local requirement for stock shelter or hay storage.

View from south side of Kentmere Reservoir, west, clockwise to north-east

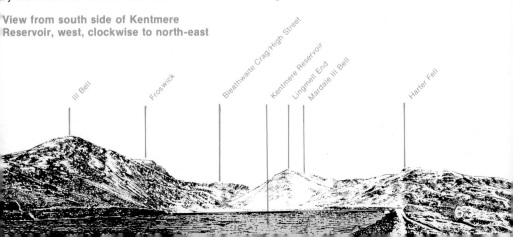

Ill Bell · Froswick · Bleathwaite Crag/High Street · Kentmere Reservoir · Lingmell End · Mardale Ill Bell · Harter Fell

Walk through the gateway just beyond the building and head south-east with a wall to your right, following the track across open fields to rejoin the river Kent. Do *not* cross the river but go left at the bridge, over more fields on a good track to Overend Farm. Go up the road and past the farm.

The flat fields below Overend Farm have produced a grass crop for at least 150 years. According to their classification after the Kendal Corn Rent Act of 1834, they bore intriguing names like Bull Meadow, Cringleton Park, Kent Bank and Boglets, and were all meadowland. In fact the majority of fields in the Kentmere valley were far too wet to grow cereals, but the hay crop must have been exceptionally good and a successful mixed beef/sheep economy flourished as a result. The number of individual fields has declined over the past century as small-holdings have been bought out by larger estates and the need for stock-proof boundaries has diminished.

Before the next group of houses and immediately after the modern sheep pen on the road, bear right off the road and onto a bridle-track, going to the left of a wall above a farm. Go through a gate and down-hill, bearing right at a junction. After about 80m, turn right again at the end of a wall, then continue along the track with a wall to your right to a little stone bridge over a small stream. Continue along the track until a larger footbridge is reached, then along a walled track through two gates.

This trackway is part of the old packhorse route that led up to Nan Bield Pass between Harter Fell and Mardale III Bell, linking the valley mills with their customers beyond. The shade from the ancient walls has enabled plants like bluebells to survive, an indication that woodland was once much more widespread.

About 100m after the second gate there are

step-stiles on either side, so neat that they are difficult to see unless you are looking for them. Go over the right-hand set and follow the path over a footbridge.

The 1836 map for the Corn Rent Act records the fields to either side of the bridge, Dalts and Bridge End Field, as pasture rather than meadow, and this area, the start of the hummocky ground of the rock bar stretching across towards Raven Crag, still has a system of small fields used for grazing. Perhaps if time has stood still anywhere in the Lake District it is here.

Continue to another walled track, turn left, past Rook Howe Farm, and follow the wide track downhill.

Rooks are not especially numerous at Rook Howe, though the trees are suitable for their nests. Farmers have always been hostile to Corvids (crows) of any sort, and although rooks balance their occasional attacks on corn against a regular diet of noxious grubs, the tradition of shooting first and thinking later probably eliminated them from here some time ago.

The small fields along the sides of the track have massive walls out of all proportion with the docile animals they are there to constrain, this time a sensible solution to what must have been a daunting problem. Faced with a million boulders (of glacial origin), prehistoric farmers started the process by clearing small patches and dumping the rocks in heaps ('clearing cairns') which were eventually translated into walls. Additional material was added by every generation for a thousand years and the fields today are free of anything weighing less than a ton. The walls are a memorial to a past tradition, commemorating (in the words of Milton) the 'labour of an age in piled stones'.

The track leads back to St Cuthbert's Church.

Overend

64

Walk Eleven
KELDAS

GLENRIDDING — KELDAS; 3km

A short walk, steep in places, through wood and fell to a fine vantage point for Ullswater and Helvellyn.

Start at Glenridding car park, GR 386169; from the car park entrance turn right over the bridge and immediately right up the lane, parallel with the stream.

Glenridding Beck draws its water from Helvellyn, via Red Tarn and Brown Cove. Heavy rain affects the current dramatically but the retaining walls are designed to cope with most floods. However, in 1927 Keppel Cove Dam burst, up above the Greenside mine at the headwater, and a wall of water 6m deep rolled down the valley. Many houses were flooded and furniture was washed across to the other side of Ullswater.

The banks of the beck are usually stable enough to be colonised by tall herbs like meadowsweet and Indian balsam, the latter growing up to 2m tall and producing curiously-shaped flowers that have earned the plant its nick-name 'policeman's helmet'. This balsam was introduced from the Himalayas about 1839 but a closely related species, called touch-me-not, is a native and a speciality of the Lake District.

Go past the Hall and between buildings as the path leads west.

The farm buildings probably date back to the 18th century, representing the later phase of the 'great rebuilding' of Lakeland farms. The transition from wattle and daub to stone structures began in Tudor times,

passing from long-house to squarer two-storey farmhouses as 'statesmen' farmers (the affluent yeoman class which had grown rich on wool) expanded their holdings and grew even more prosperous.

Continue until the path forks, at which bear left uphill past the cottages, then left through a small gate beside a five-bar gate. This leads left over a small footbridge. Bear right on the far side, then steeply to the left as the path turns steeply uphill.

Despite the gradient the ground is very marshy, the flush fed from underground springs as well as rainwater on the slopes of Keldas (the name Keldas is derived from the Old Norse 'kelda', meaning a spring or water hole). Among the alders in this damp grove are some very old ash trees, including one ancient pollard that has had its branches lopped by generations of farmers in need of tool handles or fodder for hungry stock.

Continue up the steep path through two gates.

This is the start of one of the most popular routes to Helvellyn via Striding Edge; the constant trampling and run-off of rainwater down the slope have led to severe erosion, forcing the National Park Authority to fence a broad path and criss-cross the worst section with slate bars.

Beyond the second gate bear left at the fork and continue until the path levels off.

Indian balsam

From the level ground at the top of this exhausting climb there is an excellent view of the Glenridding valley. Opposite, on the slopes of Glenridding Dodd, is a fine area of woodland — called Stibray Oaks in James Clarke's famous *Plans of the Lakes* ('Stibray' =Stybarrow). To the west, beyond the Rake, are the impressive screes beneath Sheffield Pike. In the valley itself there is some farmland, with signs of an open or common field pre-dating the enclosures, but the view is dominated by the lead-

part of mankind', capable of 'seducing and corrupting' the native population.

Continue to a gate; go through this and to the right of a small lake.

This is Lanty's Tarn ('Lanty' = Lancelot), a shallow and silty pool encircled by sedges and crowfoot and populated by midges and craneflies. The east bank is edged by a pine plantation, the west bank colonised by self-set birches. Black Crag, well-named in the afternoon shade, obscures the peak of Birk

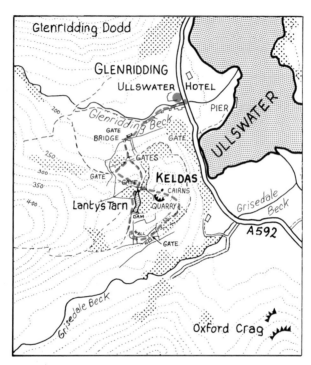

mines of Greenside which were finally worked-out in 1962 after 150 years of exploitation. This was the most productive silver-lead mine in the country; the ore (galena, ie lead sulphide) yielded 80% lead and 12 oz of silver per ton, and netted a profit of £300,000 in the fifty years prior to 1876.

Most of the terraces of miners' houses were built just over a hundred years ago, after the population of Patterdale had risen from 261 to nearly 700 between 1801 and 1851. As a community, the Patterdale miners were described by Clarke as being 'the most abandoned, wicked, and profligate

Follow the track, past a small dam, then downhill with a plantation to the left, until the track approaches a wall and bears right.

Grisedale lies ahead; the eye is drawn via St Sunday Crag to the dramatic arrête linking Helvellyn with its acolytes, Dolly-waggon Pike, High Crag and Nethermost Pike. Between the main butresses are cwms or corries, though several of them are 'dry' (ie they have not been dammed by glacial debris and do not contain tarns). The Helvellyn massif resembles Cader Idris in Snowdonia, a beautiful and awe-inspiring landscape created by ice.

Spring on Keldas, Glenridding Screes in the background

The floor of Grisedale is, by contrast, very pastoral; most of the land was once owned by the Mounsey family of Patterdale Hall who held 'considerable possessions and allodial property' in Patterdale. The family claimed direct descent via Drogo de Monseux from William the Conqueror, but the most famous Mounsey was John, 'King of Patterdale', an eccentric and notoriously mean character who is supposed to have hidden money in all sorts of strange places and probably began the decline that forced the family to sell up to the Marshalls in the early 19th century.

The track meets another, less distinct track acutely from the left: take this route, with the wall to your right, and continue to a gate. Go through this and to the left of some buildings.

Grassthwaite Howe was the stables for Patterdale Hall; all that remains of the main block are the stone pillars, but the barn and cottages are still in use.

Bear left through a gap in a wall, with the main wall now on the left. Go along the path but bear left after only 50m, off the path and through a gap in the wall. Continue obliquely uphill through light woodland, parallel with a wall to the right.

Through the trees, across the Grisedale valley, is the blunt-toothed ridge of Oxford Crag; the shallow basin between Oxford

and Arnison Crags to the east and Black Crag to the west contains Glenamara Park, encircled by an old enclosure wall with a sparse dusting of trees at its heart. Beyond Patterdale are Place Fell and Angletarn Pikes (see walk 15). Between these two imposing peaks is Boredale Hause, an obvious gap used for centuries by pedestrians on their way to Martindale. Out of view in the gap stands the Chapel in the Hause, a tiny ruin reputed to have been built by St Patrick whose name is commemorated both in Patterdale and in St Patrick's Well on the northern side of Keldas.

Follow the path, which eventually bears left uphill, away from the wall and (during summer) through deep bracken. After a few metres the path levels out with a tree-covered knoll to the right and the main hillside, and quarry spoil, to the left.

This open woodland is inhabited by green woodpeckers — the larger of the two Lakeland species. Both the green and the great spotted woodpeckers nest in tree holes, but the green is partial to ants and spends much of its time on the ground and is therefore found where there are clearings. Loud maniacal laughter earned the green woodpecker its country name of 'yaffle' or 'yapping gale'.

Turn sharp left — the route is indistinct; if the path is impossible to follow, make for the hilltop, bearing right of a small stone wall then straight ahead past an old quarry face on the left. From here go ahead up a short rocky scramble to bear left above the quarry, and so to the summit cairn.

To the west, Helvellyn is partly obscured by pine and larch trees but is still impressive; to the north-east are Glenridding and Ullswater, an unusual view of the lake as it dog-legs north with Silver Point directly opposite.

From the summit, retrace your steps for a few metres (ie towards the lake) then bear left down a gap between cairned knolls and go downhill to a fence by a wall. Continue alongside a fence, then through two fallen walls and down to a main track with the gate to Lanty's Tarn on the left. Cross the track, bearing slightly right on a wide grassy path. This rises, then falls sharply to a gate in a wall, at which bear right and along a stony path to a wicket. Continue downhill to follow the outward route back to the car park.

Keldas, looking towards Helvellyn

Old quarry on Keldas

Walk Twelve

AIRA FORCE

AIRA BECK — AIRA FORCE — DOCKRAY; 5km

The path alongside Aira Beck begins in majestic parkland and passes a series of cascades and falls, amongst them the mighty Aira Force, on its way north. The route described here includes an additional loop to the famous Victorian circuit, through the gentle farmland of Dockray and then south to rejoin the beck for a second and more dramatic view of the falls.

Park at the National Trust car park at Aira Green, 4km north-east of Glenridding on the main road: GR 401200. Leave the car park at the far side (ie north) and go up the wide track; this leads to a wicket-gate in the wall on the right.

Graceful oaks are a feature of the hillside to the left; their foliage grows outward rather than upwards, indicating that they grew as isolated parkland trees and never had to compete in a woodland canopy. By contrast, the trees beyond the wall to the right matured together and are now having to be felled one by one as they become diseased and top-heavy. Close to the path beyond the wicket are a pair of yews; the one on the right is deformed because until recently it grew alongside an oak. With the oak gone the yew is left bearing the scars of a long fight for light, and it will take centuries for it to regain its proper form. A wood is a slow-motion battleground where only the most efficient survive.

Through the wicket, follow the path to a footbridge and over a stream.

This is Aira Beck; the bridge stands in a clearing created by the death of fine specimen trees, many planted in the great age of world exploration (the late 18th – 19th centuries) when possession of such exotics as monkey puzzle became a measure of social standing — the essence of one-upmanship was to invite your neighbours around to look at a unique

Bird cherry

sapling smuggled out of Brazil or China by a quixotic adventurer.

Hidden beyond the trees to the south-east is Lyulph's Tower, a folly built at the same period. The name Lyulph is of much older lineage and the present castellated hunting lodge probably stands on the site of one built by the first Baron of Greystoke whose name, L'Ulf, is a possible root for the name Ullswater.

Go up the steps, and where the path divides bear right, up more steps.

The bank on the right faces south-west and receives whatever sunlight is available, hence there is a succession of wild flowers through the seasons: violets, pignut, heath speedwell, mouse-ear and bedstraw. A posy of violets, even as in this case the unscented sort, has always been a powerful token of love; according to classical mythology, violets sprang from the blood of Attis the tree spirit, the lover of Cybele.

Continue uphill on a wide track for several hundred metres until the path levels out and then descends.

Further up the valley, most of the big trees are either oak, beech or sweet chestnut. Only the former is a true native of Cumbria; beech was introduced from the south of England and the sweet or Spanish chestnut probably came from Italy with the Romans. To the right, beyond the fence, is open fell with a thin scatter of trees, the heart of Gowbarrow Park. Gowbarrow, once known as Wethermlake, began as a medieval deer

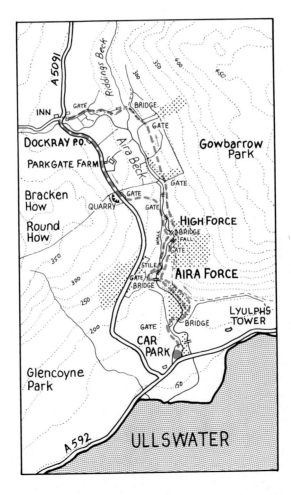

park and the estate can be traced back almost to the Norman Conquest: in the reign of Henry II it passed from the de Granthorpe family to the Barons of Dacre, and eventually by marriage to two sons of Thomas Howard, Duke of Norfolk. By the late 18th century succeeding Dukes had improved the park until its 800 hectares held up to 700 fallow deer (some estimates went much higher); there were red deer too, but enclosed parks, unlike forests and chases, were intended for the introduced fallow. These days Gowbarrow is under the protection of the National Trust and the deer are few — though some reds are reputed to swim over from Martindale.

The path leads to a bridge over the falls.

Aira Force is one of the most dramatic waterfalls in England and has inspired a rich legacy of myths and legends. The most romantic is the story of Sir Eglamore and Emma of Greystoke, who plighted their vows beneath a holly tree on this site. Immediately after this the gallant knight rode off to find fame and glory, but he timed his triumphant return badly and got back to the Tower House in the middle of the night. Etiquette dictated that he could not disturb a lady at such an hour, so he walked to the waterfall. There he discovered Emma in a deep trance, also drawn to their meeting place, and fearful for her safety he reached out to steady her. Unfortunately his touch woke her and she fell twenty or so metres to the bottom of the falls, and after a heroic rescue she died in his arms.

The shade of Sir Eglamore may still walk these woods but no-one has ever been troubled by him, presumably because he is chivalrous and has learned the consequences of creeping up on people unawares.

Do not cross the bridge, but continue up the path with the stream to your left (ignore any path off to the right). This leads eventually to a wicket-gate. Go through this and on, parallel with the stream.

The tall parkland trees are replaced here by a grove of alders and hazels, coppiced to provide a crop of brushwood — but in this case probably for the use of local tenants rather than for the charcoal, tannin or bobbin industries. This tradition obviously goes back a long way, for William Hutchinson, writing in 1794, noted that the tenants of Watermillock 'were to take by sythe; and had the privilege of *greenhue* (the cutting of brushwood) and *fern bounds* &c. the ancient *fernigo*; ferns being in much use, for bedding stalled cattle'.

At a bank above a little waterfall the path bears right, after which there is a junction with a wider path. Turn left along this new path.

The rich plant community, which includes here the curious semi-parasitic cow wheat, suggests that although the trees have been cut and managed over the centuries there has never been any attempt at clearance. The 'primary' woodland is rich not only in plants but also in bird life — green and great-spotted woodpeckers, tree-creepers,

Red deer

Aira Force. The National Trust cement-mixer and wheelbarrow belong to a conservation team

jays and flycatchers. Along the stony stream, feeding and nesting in unlikely places like the deep chasm beneath the new bridge on this stretch of Aira Beck, are large numbers of wrens. These tiny birds are responsible for the sharp, rattling songs that explode with abrupt force from the undergrowth.

Continue uphill, through open woodland to another waterfall.

This is High Force, a shelf of blue/green volcanic rock, over which in times of spate the water flows on a broad front, less tortured than on its passage further downstream. Across the beck are the fells of Bracken How and Round How, lying just outside Glencoyne Park and therefore not a part of the great enclosures of Glencoyne, Gowbarrow and Swinburn's Park. This area was once 'stinted pasture', ie tenants were able to put out a strictly limited number of animals, thereby conserving the grazing year by year.

Past the waterfall, the path leads to a gate in a wall. Go through this, through light woodland and into open fields.

Primroses

Across the enclosure wall to the right is Gowbarrow, but this area of rich grassland (rye-grass, fescue and crested dog's-tail) has been productive farmland for centuries. According to the Greystoke Estate Plan of 1778 - 1804, the two fields here on the east bank were called Miller's Park and Mounsey Field (Mounsey was the owner of Patterdale Hall), whilst the meadows on the west bank were Water-rail Close and Button Close.

Go straight ahead, on a good track, through a gate and follow the track down left and along a fence, then over a plank bridge.

The little stream, choked in the summer by water mint, monkey flowers and marsh marigold, is Riddings Beck which marks the boundary between the ancient manors of Matterdale and Newchurch. Beyond the bridge, north of the confluence of the two becks, is the Mill land, associated with old Dockray Mill.

The path leads between the cottage and barn and on to a gravelled track. Go left along the track, through the gate, and on to a road.

This is the hamlet of Dockray, comprising one large Inn (the Royal) and a cluster of one-time farm buildings and cottages.

Turn left down the A5091 Patterdale road.

A little way down the road stands Dockray Post Office, some distance from the rest of the community, a strange little building with a telephone box in the front garden. Further along the road, across a field to the left, is Parkgate Farm.

The name Parkgate is a link with the medieval history of this area, and the surrounding fields predate the main era of enclosure at the beginning of the 19th century. A contemporary record (1816) describes how 'the present duke has taken off two thirds [of the Gowbarrow estate], and converted the land into farms', but the duke retained the main deer park and also planted nearly 240 hectares of woodland. The antiquity of these older enclosures can be gauged by looking closely at the hedge on the roadside just south of the farm entrance: sycamore, dog rose, ash, hawthorn, beech and (most unusually) hornbeam, a community that took several hundred years to establish itself.

Corbie-stepped barn

Continue along the road to a lay-by on the left, opposite a small quarry.

The old estate boundary of Glencoyne is marked by the drystone wall to the north of the quarry.

Go through a wicket gate at the lower end of the lay-by and follow the path left, across a field and to the left of the rocky hummocks.

These hummocks were smoothed by glacial ice — the valley at this point is heavily dimpled by rocks worn almost flat by this irresistible force, whilst to the north and south softer material has been completely levelled and is now covered by soil. It is the outcropping that is responsible for the uneven erosion of the hillside and the development of the waterfalls over hard, resistant igneous rock.

Continue to a wicket gate above the stream; go through this and bear right.

This is High Force and Aira Beck again, but from an alternative viewpoint below the falls. A ferny place during the summer with clumps of thyme and white stonecrop, the beckside is patrolled by grey wagtails and dippers, and the open canopy of oak and elm is brought urgently to life by the song of the redstart, blackcap and wood warbler. In winter the beauty is more elemental however, a shifting balance of water or ice on bare rock.

Take the riverside path downhill to a footbridge. Do not cross this bridge but continue as before, down to a stile. Go over the stile and up to the right (ignore the stone bridge). The path levels out just before a wall is reached. Turn left down a long series of steps to cross a stone bridge below Aira Force.

This is one of the finest picture views in the Lake District, and in sunshine after heavy rain the sparkling spray and the wall of noise are breathtaking. 'Here rocks, in perpendicular and aerial splendour, recede from the eye to a vast height; but this appearance, in some instances, terrific, is in others transformed into a solemnity of beauty by trees, which impeding from the fissures of the rocks, almost exclude the light of heaven.' It must have been this sort of disorientation which, according to De Quincey, caused a Miss Smith to panic on the side of the gorge. To her surprise she saw her sister on the far bank and, through her calm guidance, was able to scramble to safety. It was only when Miss Smith reached home that she discovered her sister had been indoors all day and the silent benefactor had been conjured from the mists of her subconscious mind. Either that or it was Emma out in search of good Sir Eglamore.

Follow the path down to the footbridge you crossed on the way up; from there retrace your outward route to a wicket gate and left down the track to the car park.

Walk Thirteen
ULLSWATER

HOWTOWN — HALLIN FELL — PLACE FELL — SILVER CRAG — GLENRIDDING; 10.5km

This is not a circular route but, by starting from Glenridding and taking the lake steamer to Howtown, it is possible to walk back along the south-west shore via woods, meadows and lower fells, with out-standing views of Ullswater and mountains beyond. The distance may seem daunting but in fact the route is straightforward and has very few awkward parts. Check the times of steamers before you start; summer sailings from Glenridding were, at the time of publication, 11.30 am, 2.00 pm and 4.30 pm.

Park at GR 390169 in the car park close to the steamer pier.

Ullswater gained its first steamer (a paddle-boat called *Enterprise*) in 1859, but it was not until the Ullswater Steam Navigation Company launched its famous *Lady of the Lake* in 1877 that a passenger service began to flourish. Both *Lady* and *Raven* (brought into service at the turn of the century) were converted to oil in 1935, but they are still affectionately known as lake-land steamers.

Start the walk at GR 443199.

Once off the pier you are onto an area of flat alluvial land, its soil much richer in nutrients than the adjacent fell sides. This is reflected in the variety of trees — ash,

wych elm, sycamore, lime, alder and willow — and in the flowers like dog's mercury and ramsons which flourish on the path sides during early summer.

Bear right, along the path, over a foot-bridge and along the lake shore.

Over the fence to the left is a meadow, usually cut for hay in July. Cattle or sheep are allowed to graze most Cumbrian meadows until late winter, when they are taken off to allow the grass to recover and produce a harvest. Hayfields are rich in flowers, which go to seed before the grass is cut, but each field seems to have its own characteristic mixture. In the early summer this one is dominated by meadow butter-cup, red clover and pignut (foodplant of a pretty little day-flying moth called the chimney sweeper), with a liberal dusting of wood cranesbill and hay rattle. Beyond the meadow is the hamlet of Howtown, then the exposed ridge of Steel Knotts.

Follow the path through two wicket gates.

The shoreline of Ullswater is barren at this point due to the wave action and lack of sediment, but the water is comparatively rich, especially compared with Haweswater a few kilometres to the south-east, and has a healthy stock of perch and trout. Both Ullswater and Haweswater contain one of Britain's most local fish, known locally as the schelly or powan, a whitefish once of commercial value to seine-netters who fished these waters in the last century. Like the equally obscure vendace, a smaller whitefish which inhabits Derwent Water and Bassenthwaite Lake, the schelly relies on tiny crustaceans for its food, and so keeps out of the way of modern anglers.

At the track turn right and after about 100m turn left at a wicket gate (sign-posted Patterdale, Sandwick), and continue up the steps to another wicket. Go through this and turn right.

The steep slopes of Hallin Fell are heavily grazed by Herdwick and Swaledale sheep which prevent all but a handful of trees or shrubs from establishing themselves. Occasionally a split rock will provide an unreachable root-hold however, and in such cases the resulting tree, knarled and bent against the west wind, will probably be a rowan.

Follow the path to the left of a tall drystone wall until this ends.

May sunshine; evening light at Howtown

The wall is topped by a wire fence to prevent sheep getting into the plantation; the trees overhanging the wall are mostly oak and elm, both natural inhabitants of the area but in this case probably planted commercially. Across the lake, the woodland dome of Birk Crag is backed by Little Mell Fell.

Continue along the path which gradually bears left, parallel with the lakeside, and around the rocky outcrop of Geordie's Crag. Continue along the path into Hallinhag wood.

The name refers to a coppice, or harvested wood (a hag), on the slopes of Hallin Fell. In 1787, Clarke described it as a 'considerable grove'. The perimeter is of beech and sycamore, but these trees soon give way to sessile oaks which would have been the original crop, coppiced every few years and the shoots used for tannin. Their era is now past but the grown-out timbers remain, and these days there are many decaying trunks and stumps which offer new habitats for insects and birds.

Redstart

From May to September wood warblers and redstarts will be searching for caterpillars and flies amongst the foliage, whilst greater spotted woodpeckers will be drumming on the dead wood for beetle grubs or, if they are lucky and find an occupied nest-hole, on families of young redstarts and great tits. For the rest of the year the wood will be less hectic, most of the resident birds intent on a systematic search for seeds, and the insect-eating migrants in their African quarters.

The path through the wood keeps parallel with the lake, emerging at wicket gates in a wall. Continue into the open field; the path

leaves the lake and heads across the middle of the field making for a five-bar gate and wicket. Go through the wicket and across the next field.

To the left on the lower hillside is a ruin with a walled enclosure; in spring bluebells carpet parts of the hillside but are especially abundant within the small paddock, presumably because they have been protected from stock and sunshine since the area was cleared of its tree cover. Bluebells are woodland plants but are able to survive long after the trees have gone.

Across Ullswater rises Gowbarrow Fell, a National Trust property and the site of an ancient deer park (see walks 12 and 14).

Make for another five-bar gate and go through the wicket alongside it.

The sycamore to the left of the track is a veritable goliath, with powerful boughs and branches and beautiful flaky bark, characteristic of mature trees. Sycamore trees were introduced into Britain several hundred years ago and have proved themselves to be exceptionally fertile, robust and durable in strong winds, excellent qualities that have endeared the tree to landscape gardeners and farmers in need of stock shelter. Unfortunately birds and animals do not find the sycamore to their liking and most naturalists grow up thinking that the only good sycamore is a felled one.

Go up the track (along a line of larches) and over the bridge.

This is Sandwick Beck, drawing its water from Martindale Common. It is studded by cascades and mini-falls but is much less prone to spates or torrents than other mountain streams; this can be gauged by the fact that many of the boulders have aquatic moss (*Fontinalis*) growing on them.

Bear left up the metalled road.

The building now on the right is a 'longhouse' — a farm built so that the owner or tenant could live under the same roof as his stock. The house — whitewashed originally to prevent draughts — is on the left whilst the byre and barn are on the right. Between the two is a cross-passage marked by a door, above which is a sandstone lintel bearing a datemark, 1720, and the initials of the couple who first lived there. The barn section was not whitewashed or rendered — a throughflow of air was considered beneficial to stock. The size of stone decreases with height, a feature also true of the roof-tiles and a sign that there have been no drastic alterations over the past 250 years. Evenly-sized Welsh slates on a Lake District roof usually mean that the roof was once thatched.

Immediately beyond the building turn right, up the path signposted 'Patterdale'. Follow the path which soon changes into a track beside a tall drystone wall.

Gowbarrow still crowds the view to the right — to the left is Sleet Fell, mostly covered with coarse grass and bracken although there are some walled enclosures, intake land from the last century, providing slightly better grazing for the Herdwick sheep. Wildlife is sparse here, and the only birds likely to be seen are meadow pipits or, in the summer, cuckoos looking for meadow pipit nests.

The path descends to a footbridge over a stream, then ascends to continue alongside the wall for several hundred metres.

Insects are also infrequent on these slopes, but squashed dor beetles seem to be a regular feature along the path; dor beetles are big, fat, shiny purple/black creatures, closely related to the Egyptian scarab and very fond of dung.

On sunny summer days the grassy sides of the path contain large numbers of another purple beetle, this time a 'click' beetle called *Corymbites cupreus*. The males are very active, flying about or clambering up grass stems and waving their pectinate (ie combed) antennae about, whilst the females are busy laying eggs down among the roots (the larvae of click beetles are the infamous wireworms). Pick up a click beetle and place it upside down on your hand and it will demonstrate how it earned its name, springing itself upright and possibly off your hand by means of a trigger-release on the underside of its abdomen, producing a loud click in the process.

The wall eventually dips right, to a lane; continue along the path which contours around Roscombe Rigg, parallel with the lake shore.

Once around the promontory the view changes and the Helvellyn massif begins to dominate the skyline beyond the head of

An Ullswater steamer en route from Glenridding

the lake. The profile of the hills changes too, the slates that form the rounded hills to the north of Ullswater being replaced by much harder volcanic rocks of the Borrowdale Series, giving rise to more dramatic craggy peaks.

A little nearer, to the right of Helvellyn and its acolytes, is Watermillock Common, the lower slopes of which display an unusual (for the Lake District) profusion of hawthorn shrubs following the lines of the Swan Becks. Sheep or rabbits usually prevent this kind of regeneration.

A steady climb over several hundred metres leads to a vantage point high above the lake.

This offers what must be one of the finest

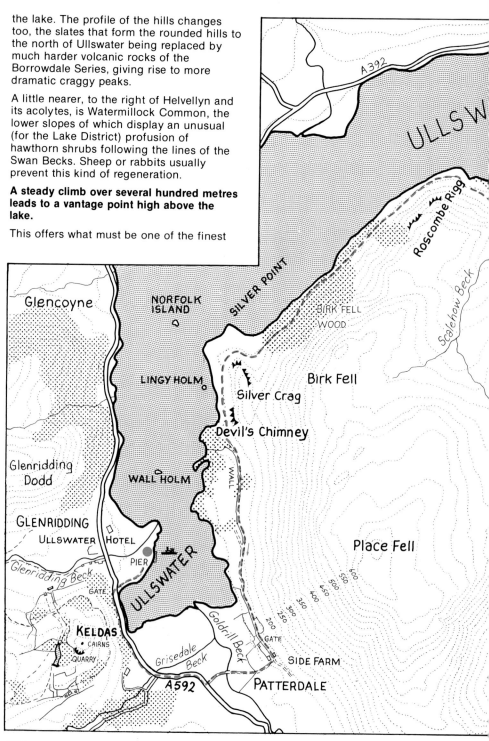

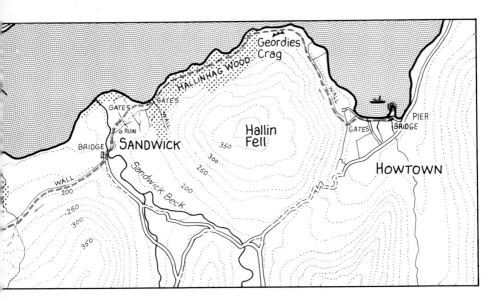

views available from any low-altitude path
in the country, made especially beautiful by
the birch woodland below Birk Fell and the
deep blue (denoting depth) of the water.
Ullswater is made up of three distinct
basins with submerged ridges or sills
between them, the first close to Geordie's
Crag and the second at Silver Point, visible
in the distance now as the lake kinks to the
south. The basins were gauged out during
the Ice Age, and the ridges — and indeed
the tiny islands — are of solid rock rather
than debris. Ullswater descends to a depth
of about 76m, but its glacier must have
been over 250m thick — an irresistible
erosive force to shape the present valley.

**Continue south-west through an area of
open woodland.**

Birch is abundant towards the lakeside, but
further up the slope of Birk Fell juniper is
the dominant tree. This is probably the
most extensive juniper forest in England, a
magical place for any naturalist interested
in what Britain must have looked like in the
years following the retreat of the ice, over
10,000 years ago. For centuries juniper
scrub was all that would grow in the arctic
climate, but eventually a host of other trees
expanded their range across Europe and
juniper was edged out, taking a final refuge
in tiny relict corners widely dispersed
throughout the country.

If you find the aromatic scent of juniper

berries or twigs familiar, think of them as
flavouring an alcoholic beverage —
preferably with tonic. In fact the French
word for juniper, 'genevrier', gave us our
word gin, and the berries were exported to
the continent for this purpose.

Birk Fell Wood is classified by the Nature
Conservancy Council as a Grade One site,
of national importance, worth more than a
cursory glance as you set off on the second
half of the walk.

**Out of the wood, the path now skirts Silver
Crag.**

Glenridding comes into view for the first
time, built on the delta of Glenridding Beck
which, with Grisedale Beck to the south,
draws its water from mighty Helvellyn. The
valleys of the becks follow fault lines,
mineral-rich and long-exploited for lead.

Two small islands attract attention; the
nearer one is Lingy Holm ('ling' is heather,
'holm' is Old Norse for an islet), with Wall
Holm in the distance. Look back down the
lake and you will find Norfolk Island,
marking the submerged ridge from Silver
Point to Glencoyne.

**The path now leaves the lake and rises past
the wooded Devil's Chimney, eventually
becoming a track with a wall to the right.**

To the left are the steep slopes of Place
Fell, ringed half way up by loose scree and
— above the scree — a collar of juniper.

81

Sorting sheep

Closer at hand are some tall larches and firs encircling an enclosure of improved pasture.

Continue along the track.

Through gaps in the wall to the right Glenridding seems a stone's throw away. Two kilometres beyond the village, back up the valley of the Glenridding Beck, are great spoil heaps from the lead mines, working until 25 years ago. The extra silt and pebbles washed downstream helped to extend the promontory on which the landing stages and pier now stand — up to 3m per year were added at the beck's outfall when the mine was at its most productive. The lead in the water was blamed for the extermination of the char, one of Ullswater's most famous fishes which disappeared from the lake in the middle of the 19th century; the employment from the mine silenced any objections from sportsmen.

The southern shore of the lake, to the left, is shallow and silty, allowing a fringe of *Phragmites* reed to flourish and providing an ideal hunting ground for herons.

Eventually the track leads to a gate; go through this towards Side Farm.

On the slopes of the fell is an old slate quarry. Local green slate was used extensively for walling but only a few of the larger quarries still survive.

The farm buildings, especially the fine bank barn to the right, demonstrate how the farm functioned in the 18th and 19th centuries. This is the back of the barn — the tall doors were built to accommodate a loaded cart. Above, there is a threshing floor which would have seen activity through many a long, hard winter as grain (usually oats or barley) was threshed by hand and the straw passed below to the byre or cow house, which has its entrance on the opposite side.

Turn right between the barn and the farm-house and walk down the track.

A lime or linden tree stands on the left, its thin leaves casting a translucent green shade. To the right is the farm yard, the front of the byre to one side, with stables (built when oxen gave way to horses in the 18th century) and other outbuildings making up the other sides of the square. Neat, functional and, as with most local architecture, perfectly in scale with the landscape.

Go.down the track and over Goldrill Beck. At the main road turn right and walk along the pavement for several hundred metres until it disappears, at which point a track leads off to the left, parallel with the road and a much pleasanter walk. Continue along this for a little over 300m.

The woodland flora, characterised by a carpet of dog's mercury, is very different to that of Birk Fell or Hallinhag, because the loamy soil is far less acidic. This innocuous-looking plant is quite poisonous; a botanic journal recorded in 1983 that an elderly couple found themselves in hospital after eating the leaves in mistake for brooklime. The journal does not elaborate on their symptoms, which is perhaps as well because Gerard's *Herbal* describes the plant as 'dangerously purgative'.

When the path ends cross the road and go through the iron gate. The path ahead leads along the lakeside to the car park and pier.

St Peter's church and Martindale from Hallin Fell

83

Walk Fourteen
HALLIN FELL

ST MARTIN'S CHURCH — HALLIN FELL; 3.5km

Martindale is often described as a forgotten valley; it is certainly beautiful and unspoiled. The short walk described here keeps to the foot of the valley (see walk number 15 for a more strenuous route to Angle Tarn via the valley head) and takes in the easy but worthwhile summit of Hallin Fell for an exceptional view of Ullswater.

Start at GR 434184; park on the grass opposite St Martin's Church (ie the old church rather than its more recent replacement, St Peter's). Cross the road and follow the grassy path to the left of the church.

The old parish of St Martin of Tours dates back 700 years, though the church was extensively rebuilt in the 16th century. Its small size and lack of an adequate congregation meant that for most of its working life it had no vicar, the stipend being too meagre. In its early years it functioned as a chapelry served by the monks of Barton, (east of Ullswater), then as a 'perpetual curacy' associated with the Vicarage of Barton. Thus the parishioners, most of them farmers and shepherds, were obliged to tackle the service themselves. It was a local statesman-farmer, Joseph Walker, who devised the first *Shepherd's Guide* in 1817, one of its rules being 'that

all stray sheep shall be proclaimed at the church on Sunday'.

These days, St Martin's is only used occasionally; in 1882 it was demoted to a 'Mortuary Chapel', but more recently it has been used on summer Sundays and on the feast day of St Martin (July 4th).

The path leads uphill, parallel to a wall on the left. Continue uphill until the wall bears sharp left.

Looking back, the site of the church was well-chosen, dominating the valley despite its small size. Its close companion, the gnarled yew (or 'crook-yowe'), is said to be 700 years old.

Because a chapel of St Martin is mentioned in 1266 it is usually thought that the valley took its name from the saint. However, Hodgson in 1820 states that 'Martindale has its name from the *martern,* an animal valuable for its fur, and which Manwood, in his treatise on the Forest Laws, first published in the reign of Queen Elizabeth, says was scarce in all other parts of England, but in this dale'. Today the pine marten is a rare animal in Cumbria, its stronghold being Grisedale Forest, 25km to the south-west.

Turn left and keep close to the wall, following the contour of the hillside for several hundred metres.

To the right are bracken-covered slopes, rising to the crags of Steel Knotts. The common nesting bird of this sort of upland country is the meadow pipit — a rather drab little creature. Among the rockier outcrops are wheatears, which often give away their position by their call, a hard 'wheet-chack', like clicking stones together.

The view to the left is of Howegrain Beck, meandering its way through the hayfields of Wintercrag Farm. Further up the valley the fields are of rough pasture, but the sheep that graze the fells and in-take land require winter feed: so the hay crop is of considerable importance. Directly across the valley above the Sessions Road (the route once used by the judiciary) and old lodge (shaded by a plantation of trees), is the ridge of Howsteadbrow; beyond this is Sleet Fell with Cat Crag at its northern end (wild cats were numerous here until the late 18th century).

Ullswater, looking north-east from the top of Hallin Fell

The wall eventually bears left. The path leads to the left of a rocky knoll, still parallel with the wall but some metres away from it.

Ahead now is Hallin Fell, and to the left the beck disappears to join Ullswater at Sandwick.

After the rock outcrop, bear left along a path until another church is reached on the right.

This is St Peter's, known locally as the New Church, built as the replacement for St Martin's and consecrated in 1882. It has modern, exceptionally beautiful stained glass.

Continue between the church and the wall to the road. Cross this and go up the grassy slope to a wall on the left; follow this uphill, and when it turns sharp left continue uphill on the wide grassy track leading slightly left.

Stop at a convenient point for a view back of Martindale and, to its right, Boredale. Both valleys show ample signs of having been sculpted by glaciers on their way to meet the major ice-mass moving north-east from the Helvellyn massif via Ullswater. Neither valley is well-wooded, and neither has very much intake or enclosed pasture on the higher ground, the area having been a deer preserve for many centuries.

After several hundred metres the broad path narrows slightly and passes through a saddle or shallow gully to a small grassy plateau. Turn right and climb to the summit cairn.

Not so much a cairn as an obelisc, about 3m tall and visible for miles around. The view from this point is quite superb: the landscape beyond Ullswater changes dramatically from west to east, at one extreme the Helvellyn range and at the

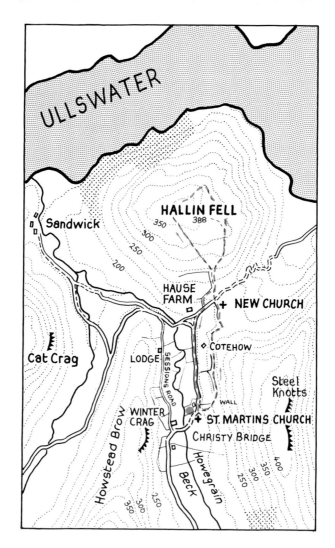

other the level plain of the river Eden with the flat-topped curtain of the Pennines beyond.

View from Hallin Fell summit, south clockwise to north-west

The geology of the area is complex, for this is where the volcanic rocks at the heart of the Lake District meet Skiddaw Slate. On

Boredale from Hallin Fell

the opposite shore, beyond Birk Crag and Hagg Wood (in the process of being re-planted), is Little Mell Fell, with Great Mell just visible to the left above Great Meldrum. The domed hills of Mell Fell are composed of conglomerate, a material rather like concrete, its pebbles culled from all the other Lakeland rocks and dumped by great floods during Carboniferous times. The flatter land to the north-east is soft red sandstone, marking the boundary of Lakeland.

The most prominent landscape feature close at hand is probably Gowbarrow, the craggy dome to the left of Meldrum. It is circled by a wall enclosing a scattered quilt of trees, indicating that it was once a deer park. To its left, across Riddings Beck is Glencoyne Park — this was an extension of Gowbarrow and it was on the shore here that Wordsworth discovered his daffodils. This also must have been the route taken by the intrepid Celia Fiennes in the 1690s. She 'rode the whole length of this water [Ullswater] by its side sometyme just by the shore and for 3 or 4 miles I rode through a fine forest or parke where was deer skipping about and hares, which by means of a good Greyhound I had a little course . .'

Leave the summit walking north-east (towards Pooley Bridge at the foot of Ullswater), passing a small cairn on the left after about 50m. Descend in the same line for about 200m through a shallow ravine.

The lower part of the lake is separated from the middle section by a distinct kink, indicating where separate basins were eroded by ice in the Pleistocene leaving a submerged ridge between Hallin Fell and the northern shore at Skelly Neb. The depth of water at the ridge is about 23m compared with 38m on either side.

At the bottom of the ravine turn right (ignore any paths immediately downhill) and follow the distinct level path for about 300m to a grassy saddle or shallow gully.

To the left is the scatter of houses known as Howtown. According to Clarke's *Survey* of 1787 'At How-Town was born James Brown who being obliged to fly his country for deer stealing, entered the army under Cromwell and was by him soon advanced to the rank of captain'. Apparently Brown made himself 'very acceptable to the Usurper by taking prisoner Sir Timothy Fetherstone at the battle of Worcester'.

Beyond Howtown are the steep slopes of Swarth Fell, where Edward Hassel (of Dalemain House, north of Pooley Bridge) led his horse down to be in at a famous fox kill. The ballad of 'Swarthfell Rocks' describes the thrill of a typical chase . . .

> They came through Howtown Moor
> Being late in the hour
> It was sometimes one hound and
>   sometimes t'other.
> It was hard to be expressed which of them
>   ran him the best
> For they each ran abreast close together

This was, apparently, the 42nd fox to meet its end at Swarth Fell, testimony to both the abundance of foxes and the diligence of the huntsmen.

Just below the saddle the path forks. Take the wider branch (steep in places) until eventually it curves right, past a low concrete structure, to join the outward route by the bottom of a wall. Follow the wall down the road, at which turn right.

The cluster of buildings to the right is Hause Farm (a hause being a gap through the hills). The gables of the main building are 'corbie-stepped', though it is doubtful if many corbies or crows have ever been allowed to walk up them.

Continue along the road to a junction, at which bear left.

To the right are the hay fields of Wintercrag, — bearing such names as Hudson Field, Hoghouse Close and The Holm — the latter meaning water-meadow and referring to the long thin field parallel to the beck. The hay is usually cut in July. A critical report on the agriculture of the county in 1805 stated that 'The hay harvest is seldom begun before the middle of June. The mowers cut from half an acre to three quarters a day, and that very ill; the hay-makers are equally indolent and inactive'. Today the operation still needs a few days' sunshine to dry the cut before it is baled, and some harvests are still lost to rain. A change to silage making is taking place on many of the larger farms.

Continue along the road southwards towards St Martin's church.

The building immediately up on the left is Cotehow, once the Star Inn, whilst a little further on, opposite the church, are the walls of an older ale house. If it is a warm day you may consider that the march of progress has not always benefitted mankind.

Fox-cub

Walk Fifteen
ANGLE TARN

ST MARTIN'S CHURCH — BANNERDALE — ANGLETARN PIKES; 11km

Martindale divides into two remote valleys, of which Bannerdale has the advantage of a recognised path at its head. The route leads south along the main valley by a little-used road (alongside which there is no parking), then obliquely up the side of Beda Fell and Heck Crag, on the slopes above Bannerdale, to beautiful Angle Tarn. The return is via Angletarn Pikes and the ridge of Beda Fell. The length and ascent may seem daunting, but in fact it is not a hard walk and is full of interest. Care should be taken on the steep section of Heck Crag and if the weather deteriorates whilst on the fell-top.

Park at GR 434184 on the grass opposite St Martin's Church (ie the old church rather than its more recent replacement, St Peter's), walk down the road and over the bridge.

Christy Bridge crosses the Howegrain Beck at the narrowest point of the valley, where it is least liable to flooding. Just across the main bridge is a smaller one over a slow, silty side stream, rich in plant life. During the spring there are patches of marsh marigold and water forget-me-not, the former bright yellow and difficult to miss, hence its plethora of names such as molly blobs and water blubbers.

By contrast, forget-me-not has small sky-blue flowers and is often overlooked, yet it has an intriguing history. It was once called snake grass, but in 1802 Coleridge wrote a poem describing it as 'Hope's gentle gem — the sweet forget-me-not', having translated the name from the German. The distinctive 'new' name then stuck. It is possible that the same plant, but known as 'soveigne vous de moy' was chosen much earlier by Henry IV and incorporated into designs and emblems for the House of Lancaster. In 1465 a collar of the flowers was the prize in a joust between two of the greatest knights of England and France, presumably as a sign or royal patronage.

Keep on the road, which bears left (south) down the valley.

To the right, on the corner, is Wintercrag Farm. Martindale once had over fifty dwellings, two inns, a corn mill, a fulling mill, and at least one bobbin mill, but now less than half of the farms and dwellings remain. In the late summer each farm

carries its own twittering crowd of fledgling swallows. It has recently been discovered that magnetism plays an important part in their navigation, and that most animals have an organic compass made up of magnetic bacteria. If so, those in a swallow's head must be particularly accurate because the birds return to the same barn every year, having completed a migration from South Africa.

To the left, the main hill-tops on the far side of the valley include Pikeawassa (level with Knicklethorns), Brownthwaite Crag and, at the end, Gowk Hill. A gowk is the local name for the cuckoo, another African migrant this time wintering in the Cameroons, which arrives on the fells during late April or May and lays its eggs in the nests of meadow pipits and pied wagtails.

Continue down the road, past Henhow (a ruin) and Thrangcrag (a small farm).

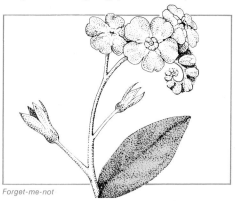

Forget-me-not

Cattle are grazed over the valley floor, particularly in the less rushy fields further upstream. Some of these may be Galloways, the rusty/black and hairy beasts that were grazed on the lower fells as long ago as the early 18th century. Better breeds like longhorns, then shorthorns and Kyloes were introduced into the Lake District in the 19th century.

The road eventually passes a private road leading to the left and continues up to Dale Head.

The private road leads away to the far fork of the valley. The red-roofed buildings are the first real clue to the tradition of Martindale as a deer forest. The top house ('The Bungalow') was for guests (the

German Kaiser once stayed there) whilst the lower house was lived in by the deer-stalker.

Deer hunting in the valley probably dates back to the de Lancaster family in the 13th century, but its survival is the result of a succession of dedicated owners. Tenants were once covenanted not to drive deer out of the valley, and according to Clarke in 1787

'the Bailiff summons all the tenants before sun-set the preceding night, to attend their strones or stations; these stations are at two places, viz. Bampskin and Bannerdale, where deer chiefly lye, and where the tenants stand with their dogs to prevent the deer escaping to the mountains. This service, which they are to render once a year, is called a *Boon Day*, and for this every tenant has his dinner and a quart of ale.'

It is curious to see the word 'forest' applied to such an open valley, but the traditional use of the term was not restricted to woodland; it was applied to an unenclosed hunting preserve to distinguish it from an enclosed 'park'. Red deer inhabited the forests, fallow deer were managed in parks.

At Dale Head turn right just before the farm gate (waymarked) and go over a stile by a wicket and turn up left, passing the farm on your left. Go over a small footbridge and up to a vehicle track, bearing right along the track with a wall on your left.

Dale Head Farm is well-situated, protected from the worst of the weather. Life on these remote farms has always been hard, especially in the 18th and 19th centuries when the value of wool fell and families worked long hours for a pitiful return. 'It is not uncommon to see, sweating at the dung cart, a girl, whose elegant features, and delicate nicely-proportioned limbs, seemingly but ill accord with such rough employment', wrote Pringle in a report to the Board of Agriculture at the turn of the 18th century. In fact, the women of Martindale must have been remarkably robust. A tradition in the dale at the first deer hunt was that whoever seized the first deer should have its head, and according to Clarke this was a woman, 'who laid hold upon him [a stag] as he stood at bay upon a dunghill, threw him down, and getting upon his neck, held him fast'.

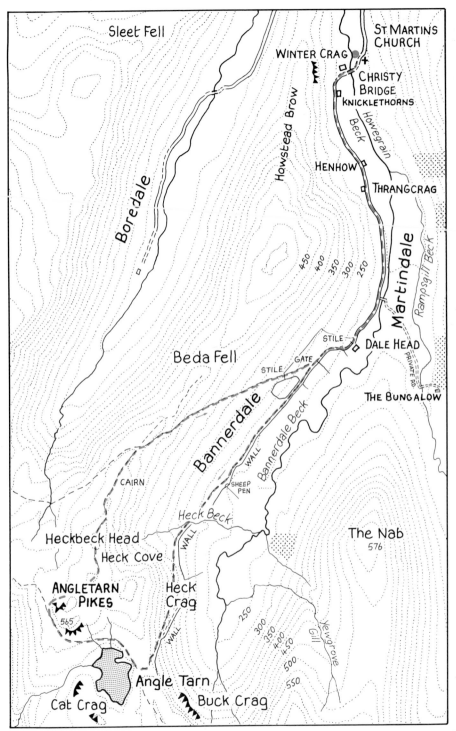

Sleet Fell

WINTER CRAG

ST MARTINS CHURCH

CHRISTY BRIDGE

KNICKLETHORNS

Howstead Brow

Howegrain Beck

Boredale

HENHOW

THRANGCRAG

450
400
350
300
250

Martindale

Rampsgill Beck

Beda Fell

STILE

DALE HEAD

GATE

STILE

PRIVATE RD

Bannerdale

THE BUNGALOW

WALL

Bannerdale Beck

CAIRN

SHEEP PEN

Heck Beck

The Nab
576

Heckbeck Head

WALL

Heck Cove

ANGLETARN PIKES

Heck Crag

WALL

250
300
350
400
450
500

Yewgrove Gill

565

550

Cat Crag

Angle Tarn

Buck Crag

Across the valley, the great wedge of fell that once separated two arms of a glacier now rises abruptly to The Nab.

In about 200m the track divides. Keep left by the wall to a gate; go through this, keeping to the same line.

The ruin to the left was probably a barn for storing hay but has also been used to house stock. This can be deduced from the abundance of nettles which require a lot of nitrogen and phosphate and so do well wherever there is a build-up of organic matter. There is a lot of willowherb too (an indicator of disturbed ground) and both creeping and spear thistle. The latter are in flower in August, when their nectar attracts small tortoiseshell and peacock butterflies away from egg-laying duties on the nettles.

Continue to a small walled enclosure by the fell wall.

The semi-circular walled enclosure is an ingenious sheep pen, designed to gather flocks from either direction using a minimum of gates. These days most of the sheep are Swaledales, or crosses thereof.

Here the path veers right a little, still parallel with the wall to join it again in about 300m.

The terrain is very much more rocky here, a suitable nesting area for wheatears which like to hunt for insects on the short turf.

In a west wind this side of the valley is very well protected, but if there is a shift to the north Bannerdale acts like a funnel and the breeze can turn to an arctic gale.

Continue up the steep path (main wall on the left) until level with a ruined wall to the right.

View from north summit of Angletarn Pikes, south-east clockwise to north-west.

Kestrels are regularly seen hunting on the slopes, but the site is so wild and remote that there is a good chance of peregrines too. The changes in the populations of birds of prey in these uplands is quite remarkable. The red kite was once common around Ullswater and both golden and white-tailed eagles had eyries in the major valleys. But eagles were fond of lambs and their systematic extermination was inevitable.

The Rev. W. Richardson noted that 'a pair of the Golden Eagles had an eyrie in Martindale [close to this point] two successive years: the first year the female was shot, and the male, after an absence of about three weeks, returned with another female. The next year, in 1789, the male was killed, after which the female disappeared'. There has been no attempt to nest here since then. Eagles have returned to the eastern Lake District and seem to be doing well, however, so there is always a chance of seeing one hunting the fells, especially during the winter when they range over a wide area.

The red kite or glead was so thoroughly eliminated from England and Scotland that there is little hope of its return for some time yet, but the peregrine, having gone through a disastrous decline due to pesticides rather than persecution, is now widespread.

The path divides at this point: take the right-hand higher fork — it is easier and there is no loss of height, though the paths rejoin after a few hundred metres.

The scree slopes below Heck Crag are an interesting place to linger, dramatic but dangerous if you stray from the path.

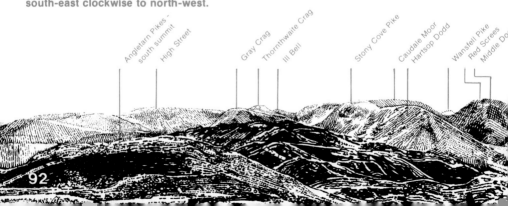

Alpine lady's mantle, parsley fern and saxifrage, hidden amongst the glacial debris, are among those plants that have adapted to the difficult, unstable conditions.

Looking back down Bannerdale, Heck Beck appears as a nick or line in the levelling slope to the left of the valley; just beyond this, on a grassy promontory close to the enclosure wall, is an ancient British settlement. This tribe was probably the first community to call Bannerdale home, and they chose the site well; any further up the valley and the midsummer sun would have disappeared at tea-time!

Continue alongside the wall for another 200m, then follow the path as it bears right, away from the wall, to cross a little grassy col or dip in the line of the hill.

The change of view comes as a surprise; suddenly Bannerdale is gone and before you is Angle Tarn and a panorama of mountains, of which the cone of Catstycam ('Catstye Cam' according to the 1:25,000 map) is the most distinctive. To the left is Swirral Edge leading to Helvellyn and, completing the horse-shoe, Striding Edge. If you are finding this walk easier than you expected then the Helvellyn ridge is something to aspire to, one of the most impressive mountain walks in England.

Just the other side of Angle Tarn is Cat Crag, whilst up to the south (left) is Brock Crags. This part of the Lake District has several Cat Crags, dating back at least to the 18th century when the wild cat was still numerous. Often, animals' names were applied to places following memorable hunts, and since a total of twelve wild cats were killed around Ullswater in a single week in the spring of 1759 it is surprising that more were not immortalised in this

way. Badgers were less common because the habitat was not so suitable, but there are Brock Crags both here and on Beda Fell to the north, suggesting there must once have been a healthy population with setts in the valley woods.

Turn right on a wide path that skirts the tarn.

For its size Angle Tarn is shallow, descending to a maximum of about 9m towards Cat Crag. Apart from a few birches in places sheep cannot reach, the vegation on the banks is short and sparse, a feature of most of the higher mountain tarns (you are at an altitude of about 480m). Emergent plants — that is, ones that grow in the water but push their leaves or flowers well above the surface — have colonised the sheltered southern bays. Bottle sedge and water horsetail are abundant, with a few patches of water lobelia, easily overlooked until its delicate flowers appear in mid to late summer.

Follow the path past the tarn until a small path bears up to the right. This leads around the southern summit of the Pikes. Keep this to your right and continue until you are alongside the northern summit. Leave the path by the cairns and turn sharp right, up the grassy slope, and then up a little gully which leads to the rocky summit of Angletarn Pike and a cairn.

The view is spectacular to the west but also interesting to the south-east, where a screen of hunch-backed giants — High Raise, Rampsgill Head and High Street — hide Haweswater and the lower eastern fells. The small square lake to the south-west is Brothers Water: Dorothy Wordsworth wrote of 'the gentle flowing of the stream, the glittering lively lake, green

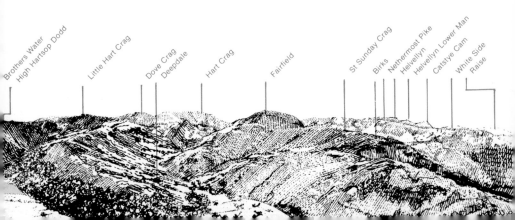

Brothers Water · High Hartsop Dodd · Little Hart Crag · Dove Crag · Deepdale · Hart Crag · Fairfield · St Sunday Crag · Birks · Nethermost Pike · Helvellyn · Helvellyn Lower Man · Catstye Cam · White Side · Raise

Golden eagle

Go forward past the cairn to the end of the grassy summit ridge. Bear right, downhill for about 20m. Care is needed now as there is no path for several hundred metres; with your back to the summit make for the grassy knoll about 250m ahead.

This lonely knoll is a favourite place for sheep, possibly because the top of it has a little patch of palatable grass. The lower slopes are covered in mat-grass with extensive patches of heath rush, of little grazing value but a characteristic plant community of the high fells.

From the knoll bear left (north) for 200m to reach a path. Continue along this, following the grassy ridge.

The head and foot of Ullswater are so far apart (12km) that they look as if they must be joined to different lakes. Between them are, from the right, Beda Fell (on which you are standing), Hallin Fell (see walk 14) and Place Fell. To the left of the latter, and across Patterdale and the southern end of Ullswater, are the valleys of Grisedale and Glenridding. The dip in front of Place Fell is Boredale Hause, in which is situated the 'Chapel in the Hause', a small building constructed, according to local tradition, by St Patrick in the 5th century to establish the cult of St Martin of Tours.

A pair of ravens is usually to be seen above Beda Fell, and this is a good place to stop and listen for their throaty calls and watch their aerobatics. Ravens were heavily persecuted because they were thought to kill lambs, and at one time there was a tradition of hanging their heads on the yew tree of Martindale Church. Today they are still in trouble with some farmers, which is why they keep high up on the fells.

Continue to a large cairn, then on for another 300m to a small cairn in a grassy saddle or dip, marking a path crossroads.

Look for red deer on The Nab; in summer when they retreat to the high hills they can sometimes be seen browsing below the summit peat-haggs on the brow of Yewgrove Gill. At first, pick out the little white dots (sheep), then look for a group of larger brown dots moving more quickly. It often takes a few minutes to locate a herd but it is satisfying to have found them, even

fields without a living creature to be seen on them'.

Beyond Brothers Water is Hartsop Dodd, wedged between Dovedale to the right and Kirkstone Pass to the left. On its lower slopes is another ancient settlement of similar age to that in Bannerdale, and it is an intriguing possibility that the Roman road of High Street, linking the peaks mentioned above, was constructed with an eye to isolating these communities from

Swaledale ewe and lamb

at such extreme range. The deer of Martindale, numbering two or three hundred in total, are from truly wild stock and have never been enclosed.

Leave the ridge path and go right, downhill. The path slants north down into Bannerdale and past a ruined building. Follow the obvious path down for almost a kilometre to a stile by a gate. Go over this and continue downhill in the same line to join the outward route just above Dale Farm. Retrace your outward path by skirting the farm on the left, over the footbridge and stile to join the road, then back along the road.

*If you have enjoyed these walks don't hang up your boots:
companion volumes include WALKS TO REMEMBER –
NORTHERN LAKE DISTRICT and WALKS TO REMEMBER
– SOUTH AND WEST LAKE DISTRICT*

Published by
Polecat Press Ltd
Registered Office
63 High Bridge
Newcastle Upon Tyne
NE1 1DU